Some Mothers I Know

Also by Tom Wakefield

Special School
Trixie Trash, Star Ascending (novel)

Some Mothers I Know

Living with Handicapped Children

Tom Wakefield

Routledge & Kegan Paul
London, Henley and Boston

First published in 1978
by Routledge & Kegan Paul Ltd
39 Store Street,
London WC1E 7DD
Broadway House,
Newtown Road,
Henley-on-Thames,
Oxon RG9 1EN and
9 Park Street,
Boston, Mass. 02108, USA
Set in 11 on 12pt Old Style (Series 2)
by HBM Typesetting Ltd
Chorley, Lancs.
and printed in Great Britain by
Lowe & Brydone Printers Limited,
Thetford, Norfolk

ISBN 0 7100 8783 7

For two doctors and a doctor's wife:
Dr Marie Roe, Dr Mary Wilson
and Mrs June Franklin

Contents

	Preface	xi
1	May Hudson	1
2	Babs Wilson	17
3	Rose Seward	39
4	Margaret Estelle Gates	57
	Beginning	83

It seemed to me that it would be a base thing for me to slip out of the world leaving it out there all alone, waiting for its fate – that would never come!

Sentiment, pure sentiment as you see, prompted me in the last instance to face the hazards of that return. As I moved slowly towards the abandoned body of the tale it loomed up big amongst the glittering shallows of the coast, lonely but not forbidding. There was nothing about it of a grim derelict. It had an air of expectant life. One after another I made out the familiar faces watching my approach with faint smiles of amused recognition. They had known well enough that I was bound to come back to them. But their eyes met mine seriously, as was only to be expected since I, myself, felt very serious as I stood amongst them again after years of absence. At once, without wasting words we went to work together on our renewed life and every moment I felt more strongly that they who had waited bore no grudge.

Joseph Conrad
(Author's Note to 'The Rescue' 1920)

Preface

'Write a book about us,' they said to me. 'You've heard plenty, we will tell you more. You have known us long enough, it's not as though you will be just clicking a tape recorder on and off, is it?'

'There have been other studies on this subject,' I said.

'Yes, but can everyone understand them? I've tried to read some of those books. All charts and tables – have to put them down, gave me the headache.'

I thought of some of the books, and in all fairness chose to defend them.

'A book like this has to be objective, things have to be recorded and noted as you go along. Opinions have to be related to research. Retrospect or "looking back" is not always considered reliable.'

'Oh, you sound like those people who spend thousands of pounds predicting elections. They're not always right are they? Anyway, you don't have to be right, try to get across how we feel. Isn't that what writing is about? You could do that for us, we can talk. We will help you.'

I evaded them.

'It would be subjective,' I said.

'What?'

'I am biased. I know you all too well. It would be a book with too much of me in it when it is supposed to be all about you. However much I try to avoid it, what I write will be decided by me and not entirely by you. This is not fair, it might make me seem better or nicer than I really am. People will say it is an egocentric account, this means that I might be just eating your experiences to answer my own needs.'

'So what? You are not afraid are you?'

'When I am working with you, no, I'm not. Each day is a day, and that is that. A mistake or a motive for helping or a search for asking for help is swallowed up and lost by doing. Writing is different.' I faltered.

'We understand that, don't we Babs? You're not afraid are you? You can't be.'

'He is a bit, perhaps a lot. Those fears are useless. Say "I" if you want to say it. Don't you change my name, spell it out in full. Nobody will want to judge what we say, just let them read it. It's our book and yours, leave it at that. You're not proud.'

'Thanks,' I said, hoping that this last statement was true.

'Will you enjoy doing it?'

'I don't know, I don't know.' . . . Anita, June, Enid, Babs, Maggie, Rose, Rita, May, Molly, Clare – who do I select, where do I begin? It might be wise to maintain this bewilderment and confusion and substitute it for any objectivity that may creep in.

1
May Hudson

'It was June. I remember it because I have always worked and when you are working you can't really appreciate a warm summer's day, or notice it for that matter. You don't have time, do you? My Freddie was eighteen months and being at home with him was a luxury for me. I'd pushed his pram to the top of the garden and put a net over the canopy because I'd heard stories of cats attacking babies – when you only have one baby I suppose you're extra careful. The garden was full of vegetables coming through, Londoners grew more vegetables in those days and I was glad to see it all neat. I went in to finish some washing – it was warm enough to dry in an hour and it seemed sensible to take advantage of the weather.

'The clothes basket was on the table and I had gone into the scullery for my peg-bag. It was then that I heard the scream, perhaps it seemed louder than it was because it was summer and everything was warm and still. Perhaps it seemed louder because I knew it was from my baby. That scream went right through me. I never stopped to dry my hands. Cats, cats I thought. One has gone for him. I was terrified but I ran out into the garden as fast as I could. Being frightened for your baby is much worse than being frightened for yourself, you know.

'There were no cats anywhere and the net of the canopy was still there. I lifted the net, I knew that something terrible had happened because of the smell, there was sick everywhere and the counterpane was covered with it. Then I noticed Freddie's eyes – usually they were full of fun. Alive you might say. His eyes were glassy and they stared at the sky. I picked him up and tried to get a response from him but all I got was this staring. I put him back in the pram and fetched my neighbour who lived in the flat above me. When I think back about it this was probably wrong of me because she was pregnant at the time. She held him for me while I got a blanket to wrap round him. His head lolled to one side and he was still staring. I never cried, I think I was too shocked for tears – all I could think of was to get him to the doctor's as quickly as possible. Fortunately, the doctor lived near, but the hundred yards' walk still seemed like the longest walk I have ever taken in my life. The surgery was closed and I banged and hammered the front door with my fist.

'Thank God, the doctor opened the door and let me in. He could see I was desperate I suppose. As we sat down Freddie vomited again. The doctor looked at me and frowned, "What the hell have you given him to eat?" "I've just given him his normal feed. Will he be all right?" The doctor answered me by telephoning for an ambulance and as he phoned Freddie was sick again.

'When we arrived at the Eastern Hospital I had the feeling that it was a nightmare and that I would wake up and it would be over. They took Freddie from me and after about an hour a sister came to see me. "I'm sorry Mrs Hudson, we think that Freddie might have some form of encephalitis. We are measuring his head and taking some tests, but it will mean that he might have to stay with us for a few days." "Would it affect – would it affect his brain?" I said. "Yes there would be a possibility of some damage but we are not sure. We have contacted your husband at work and he's coming over to collect you." "It's serious then," I said and I remember holding the sides of the chair as I sat down. "I'm afraid it could be Mrs Hudson, yes." Then I cried. I cried really hard and I didn't, couldn't care less who watched me.

'My husband came to me straight from work and two doctors saw us straight together and asked some questions.
1. Had your baby ever had a heavy fall?
It's funny when people ask you questions like this, in this kind of situation, your mind goes a blank – I kept trying to remember, but I found it difficult to concentrate. I felt as if bits of me

2

were going off in all directions. It was Ernie my husband who reminded me that Freddie had knocked his head on a gate-leg table – but it had been months before and there was only the tiniest of marks left on his forehead.

2. What about the birth? The actual birth itself, did you have a difficult time, was the labour long? Were there any particular problems?

As a matter of fact there was no problem at all as it was a Caesarian birth, it was as simple as having a couple of teeth out and less painful. All I could remember was being pregnant and childless one minute and looking down at my son the next. The hospital didn't come to any definite decisions. I remember they measured and muttered that it might be encephalitis; he had been a lively baby and in my heart I thought they were wrong about that. By late evening he was right as rain and they said it was all right to take him home. Ernie and me were so relieved we took a taxi home and that was very extravagant in those days.'

The most striking thing about May Hudson is her realism – even when she is being humorous (and this is often) she manages to extract by the truthfulness and clarity of her expression more than in contrived witticisms. Once when she told me she was going abroad for her holidays I expressed muted surprise. In answer to this she did a samba around the bench in the playground and sang, 'I'm going Pontinental, I'm going Pontinental' and finished it off with an 'olé'. It is strange that I had known and worked with May for more than eight years before she gave me any indication that her son was handicapped. When she finally broached the subject she apologised for burdening me with it – 'I know you have enough on your plate here.' My plate was clear compared with what had been cleaned from hers.

'As he was our only child, we were extra careful with him, we were so thankful that he was back with us with nothing wrong. We were a bit worried because he often rocked himself and would go as if to bang his head against the wall. I felt it must have been headaches, because when I have a throbbing headache that's what I feel like doing, don't you? I don't do it because I know it won't do anything to lessen the headache, but an eighteen-month-old baby isn't to know that, is he? I told them about this when I next visited the hospital but they just

3

measured his head again and said it was nothing to worry about.

'One night (in fact it must have been two in the morning because I was always getting up to see if he was all right) this night I can remember because I could smell the sick before I reached the cot. It was just like a nightmare in the early hours of the morning, the coverlet and bedclothes were covered in vomit and bile, his little face was pulled and drawn and his eyes couldn't see me because they were glassy as they had been before – he was just staring up at the ceiling. Ernie went round for the doctor, he came round straight away, he was a good man. He had no airs or graces. Do you know that doctor ran round my home with Ernie without wasting a minute. He was wearing dirty plimsolls, he was a very kind, very real man.

'In the meantime Freddie had begun to retch; convulse is the proper word. I know all the terms now. I turned him on his side, the doctor muttered "Ambulance" and we were at the Eastern Hospital fifteen minutes later. Freddie remained unconscious for five or six hours just like the time before.

'They kept him in hospital for two weeks' observation; at the end of this period the sister saw me in her office. She spoke to me as if she was announcing a weather forecast: "Mrs Hudson we have every reason to believe that your son is suffering from epilepsy. Freddie is an epileptic."

'I had a vague notion what epilepsy was and I had seen one or two people have what I knew was a fit, but I never thought it could happen to my family. We were only a small family anyway. "Oh," was all I could say to the sister. I thought, "Why should this happen to me?" Yet it had happened and after this he was transferred to Queen Elizabeth Hospital. He was sent home again, but every ten weeks the attacks came back regular as clockwork. On one occasion when he went over the usual time the sister had wondered what had happened to him, she said she'd missed him. I suppose it was funny in a grim sort of way. Epilepsy had now definitely been confirmed – I had got used to the procedure by now and I even held the oxygen mask for him in the ambulance. This went on for another four years before I realised, without thinking about it too much, that I was having to live with my son's illness in much the same way as he was having to grow in spite of it. I suppose that's why I made an effort to know a bit more about epilepsy. I don't suppose I would have bothered otherwise. How many people would know, I mean if you just went round while you were shopping and you asked them what a convulsion was, or a Petit Mal or a Grand Mal? I know they are only names but people get a wrong impression if they don't know about things. I know once, I saw a poor man on the platform of the tube station and people had gathered round him, nobody had knelt near him or loosened his tie, or turned him on his side or done anything practical to help. One man with a brief-case shouted to the ticket office, "It's drugs, drugs – telephone the police, the travelling public have a right to go to work in peace."

'Normally, I'm the sort that minds its own business, I knew what to do and knelt with the poor bloke on the floor after I had said that it was an ambulance that was needed. I did give the man with the brief-case a bit of a mouthful – and felt a bit bad about what I had said to him afterwards. But, then again, I could forgive his ignorance but not his bloody selfishness. A few people stayed with me until the ambulance arrived and the man was beginning to recover a little by then. I just left the situation, I couldn't do no more, and went to work as if nothing had happened. I suppose it's easier to accept things like that if you've had it on your own plate. I don't expect everybody to be aware – but sometimes they are downright bloody cruel. I'll always remember that brief-case – the man had a striped tie with a little knot. I've forgotten what his face looked like. Some things you learn to forget (like his face).' May laughed and continued: 'Other things you learn to accept like my Freddie's illness, accepting things cuts out a lot of worry you know.

'We had a lot to worry about in them days, you see we only had a basement flat, just two rooms and a scullery, and money wasn't easy to come by. Ernie and me both worked during the three years before Freddie was born. Of course after Freddie came I had to give up work and it was a struggle to manage. A handicapped kiddy is more expensive than one that isn't, not just in time and care but in expenses too. Anyway we struggled and managed. Looking back only God knows how. Although, it brought me and my husband much closer to each other you know, we are not just man and wife by law. We are really close friends who trust one another completely and in a way we can thank Freddie for that. I have no regrets about my son being with us nor do I feel hard done to now. In fact, me and Ernie have a lot to thank him for.' May lit a cigarette, offered me one and took a puff at hers.

'I'm a Catholic you know, not a very good one, Ernie isn't but that hasn't made a difference to our marriage. Except that in my case praying a bit has often helped me.' May looked at me as I was rummaging in my pockets. She lit my cigarette for me. 'Does that surprise you?' she asked.

'You've always surprised me, May.' We laughed, she talked on through the chortles and sniggers.

'I have a lot to be thankful for. I met Ernie quite late in life by modern standards (or even as things were then) and married him quietly soon after we met. We have gone on together ever since – quietly – we like a bit of fun from time to time but for the most part we are quiet and happy.

'You see in the early part of our marriage we couldn't go out, it was a case of having friends visit us as we didn't want to take Freddie out too far away from the hospital who knew his history. I must say, once the epilepsy was confirmed the hospital saw him and tested him as regular as clockwork, they were most careful. They introduced him to a drug which they said would control the fits and by the time he was three years old, it seemed that he wasn't subject to fits any more. He had gone for almost a year without a fit and we felt blessed, I can tell you that. We were very conscientious giving him his tablets and felt ever so much less anxious about going out with him. In any event we felt that we should now treat him as normally as possible and we took him out with us when we visited friends. By the time he was four we felt completely relaxed. I remember we had gone over to friends for tea – they lived in Finsbury. We were having a good time, I think we were playing cards and Freddie was playing with my friends' children.

' "There's something wrong with Freddie." It was one of their children who shouted to us, we were talking in the lounge. We had learned to keep calm and move quickly, we got our son to the nearest hospital – this was the Middlesex in Goodge Street. When we got there they said the fit would probably only last a few minutes, but it turned out to be much longer. The hospital still kept in touch with us when Freddie recovered. They also asked about any trace of epilepsy in my family and Ernie's – but we traced all our relatives as far back as we could and found none. A few weeks later they did more tests on Freddie and found the outer wall or lining of his brain was slightly damaged. However, they were very comforting and kind and said that this was unlikely to affect Freddie educationally. Six months passed by and Freddie was not affected by the Grand Mal we had now come to dread. In fact the Middlesex Hospital were so confident about treatment they said that a placement in a nursery school would help him. They said they would arrange an interview, and good as their word a note came asking me to take Freddie for an appointment as regards admission to a local nursery school.

'On the day of my interview at the school it was me that was surprised. I can laugh about it now but at the time I felt so embarassed. The headmistress showed me into her room (she was a nice lady) and she said "Hello" to Freddie. He responded normally but do you know he would not sit down, he was buzzing around that room like a bee looking for honey. There were lots of little toys and knick-knacks on the cupboards and shelves and he went from one to another, no sooner had he picked one thing up than he cast it down and went on to the next. I got quite firm with him, as I had never seen him like this before. "Freddie, Freddie," I said, "come here, play with just one of the things and I can talk to the lady." He wouldn't come. It was impossible to go on with the interview and I could see that the headmistress felt as sorry for me as I did for her. You know how busy headteachers are? She said he appeared to be hyper – er – something or other.'

'Hyperkinetic.'

'Yes that's it, it means that a child is always on the move, restless-like and can't concentrate.

'She must have seen how upset I looked and said, "Look, I'll keep a place open for him, Mrs Hudson, bring him back in a month's time. None of the notes say that he behaves in this way, perhaps you can get him used to the idea gradually about coming here. Walk past the building and point to it. Get some other children to play with him more at home. He is probably just over-excited because he's not been able to have the ordinary kind of play that children not suffering from any handicap are entitled to by nature immediately after they are born." I felt a lot better when she had said that and I could tell by the expression on her face that she was not going to reject my little boy. Those are the faces you remember aren't they?'

I looked at May's face. The make-up (lightly applied) could not hide some of the lines, but age had not diminished her innate buoyancy and good will. The auburn rinse in the hair highlighted the sparkling green eyes and somehow her white knee-length boots, which might have looked incongruous on some other women of her age, suited her splendidly. She would always go forward taking on any hurdle. She broke my reverie.

'Now what are you thinking about?' she asked.

'I was thinking about your face, May,' I said. She laughed, loud and long and I joined her. At the time of writing this May is being employed as a woman helper in an ILEA special school. She was commonly known as everybody's mum, staff included. May emanated comfort in the way that most people breathe. She continued to talk.

'Well, my face could hardly earn me my fortune. I've always had to work you know. I was in the print first of all, and I drove an ambulance during the war. I never thought I could ever learn to drive but I did, didn't I? You see I'd seen a lot of life before I had Freddie; he was a bit of a spectacular because somehow I hadn't expected a baby after so long. I know that Ernie was pleased when I was expectant – but our baby brought us closer together, I mean marriage isn't all sex is it? Mind you I haven't done without it – but it's better if you're close friends you know. It's part of everything then and it's often the quickest way to settle a silly row or quarrel. And Ernie's always been very good you know, he'll help out at home and always gave us all the support he could.'

'Would you support Women's Lib then, May?'

'Well, darlin', I suppose it's the luck of the draw with men. I've always felt to be on equal terms with my husband and we have always shared the problems that some women seem to have to take on their own. Perhaps it might have been different if we hadn't have had so much initial trouble with Freddie. I don't know. It would have been hell if Ernie hadn't been as good as he is. I think women should be given all the chances offered to men, but they must stay women if you see what I mean.

8

'They did take Freddie in at the nursery, the headmistress took him in eventually, her suggestion as to getting him in school worked, the second time I took him for interview he went in like a duck to water without a bit of bother. I discussed his behaviour at the first interview with my husband. We were puzzled about it because when we took him to the hospital for his check-ups he became still and quiet as a stone, almost as though he wasn't with us or as if he wasn't there.'

'Withdrawn?'

'Yes.'

'I've heard you use the word before.'

'I suppose the hospital, however friendly, only meant one thing for him and he didn't like going there any more than we did. He didn't see school in the same light, and all the teachers seemed to like him. He was very well behaved, I think too well behaved in a way.'

'What do you mean?'

'Well, he never gave any trouble, I mean in behaviour, but he was a bit behind, just that bit behind the others. I was so relieved about the fits decreasing I didn't think about it too much at the time. His regular dosage of phenobarbitone seemed to have done the trick because we saw no more fits and he sailed through nursery school without having any more attacks. By the time he was seven and attending an ordinary infants' school I felt confident enough to get a part-time job myself. It was as a helper in the school kitchen, this meant he wouldn't miss me at the usual times, and to be honest we needed the money because we had got better accommodation. More rent, but you have no idea what an extra bedroom can mean after you have lived in cramped surroundings. The hospital were as happy as we were, and at eight they suggested we try to wean him away from the drugs, just decreasing the dosage gradually. We got it down to nil and it felt like the "all clear" during the blitz. I don't suppose you would remember that kind of relief. It's a marvellous feeling.'

May's look reflected the kind of acceptance and anguish that one sees amongst women depicted on a medieval pietà – the head held slightly on one side, the sorrow there in abundance, but no alarm, a studied calm, replacing what might have been despondence in other women.

'Yes,' she sighed, and pondered over the single word. 'It was during this period when he had his very worst fit. It happened at school and they got him to hospital as quickly as possible. I was informed immediately and arrived at the hospital not many minutes after Freddie had been admitted. After three hours he was still not conscious and he received an injection which helped him to recover from the fit. He was back at school again within a matter of days, but we have never risked forsaking his tablets since that time, nor have the hospital suggested that we should.

'Freddie was very happy at the primary stage of his education too; you see the infants were combined with the junior children so it meant that there was no uneasy change in his surroundings – he was always looking forward to each school day during this period and I think he progressed very well in this environment, as well as enjoying it. At times he became a bit over-active but the teachers said this was periodic and he took part in all the activities that went on. In his attainments he was just below average compared with the other children; considering what he had been through we didn't feel that we could grumble about that. Far from it, all the class teachers had given him all the help they could and when he reached secondary age he was stable, he had some good friends and playmates and school held no fears for him. Like most of the children in his school at eleven-plus Freddie was transferred to one of the local secondary schools. Do you know, I was more thrilled and excited than he was when I took him shopping for his school uniform, we had got this far and to all intent my son was entering what would probably be the last part of his time at school. Oh, I did feel proud of him when he left for the "big" school on his first day. Just after he started there was when I first met you.

'I heard of guiding from a friend of mine and made some enquiries about the job. I can't remember much about the interview, I was just myself. It must have suited the headmistress because I was given the job as a "guide". Anyone just hearing that description would think it was to do with leading someone or helping the blind. As you know, blindness never came into it, but I suppose there are more ways of "guiding" children than just taking them by the hand.'

It was during this period that I first encountered May Hudson. It was my first teaching post in a day school for maladjusted children. The school was all-age from five to sixteen years and catered for children who were emotionally disturbed to the extent that they could not be educated in an ordinary school. The degree of disturbance varied and it was necessary for some children to be escorted to and from school by women of sympathy and understanding like May. The headmistress of the school seemed to have an extraordinary ability in finding just the women who were needed for such a task. It was by no means an easy one, and these 'guides', as they were then known, must have been motivated by compassion to do the work they did because the salary for the responsibility involved was miserable. The maximum number of children on roll at the school was never beyond fifty pupils, and in these therapeutic surroundings all adults and children involved in the building got to know and understand one another probably more than is usual in any other kind of working situation. May was regarded as something of a stalwart, as she was responsible for guiding Johnny. His emotional disorders manifested themselves in patterns of behaviour which could make the most experienced of teachers in this field despair. May smiled her way through it all and accepted and waited – and I believe made an enormous contribution to Johnny's eventual improvement and adjustment. Again May's humour drove her on to talk more; she laughed.

'Oh, I'll never forget Johnny, no never, how could I?'

'Neither could I May,' I said, as I ruminated over bruised shins that any footballer might have been proud of. They were accepted in much the same way by the recipient at the time – just part of the game which one hoped would eventually end as the play improved.

'He still calls round at my house to see me you know, now that he is grown up. He's ever so smart and really handsome, quite the little gentleman, I couldn't quite believe that he would turn out so well you know, he'll even talk about some of the terrible times he gave me. We laugh about it together now.

'Once on the bus, he gave me a very bad time. You see we had to make a change in the usual route. It was quite simple really. The bus stopped and we were all told it was going no further. This sometimes happens you know and they never give you a reason. Everybody grumbled a bit and began to pile off the bus to wait for the next. Not Johnny, he wouldn't budge. The conductor came up and started to shout and that did it. Johnny turned on me, he called me all the names under the sun, you name 'em he shouted them. The conductor just shot back down the stairs as he could see what a temper the boy was in. The people on the pavement looked up, if there was a way of helping none of them could have offered much.

'Fortunately, he was sitting on the inside seat and I let him rip good and proper for a few minutes, it seemed longer though. Then I took his hand and held it, with all the screaming and shouting he had tired himself out. Then he began to cry. I had seen him do this before so I knew the pattern. I put my arm around him and gave him a bit of a cuddle (just like you do with a baby of two or three) and I said, "Come on now Johnny, you don't want all those people in the queue seeing you like that." He got over it. I wiped his tears and we joined the rest of the passengers in the queue as if nothing had happened. Some of them gave me some miserable looks, as though it were my fault, but I've no time for those kind of stares and as I had seen them before on account of my own son they didn't give me one second of worry.

'When I think it over now I really believe that children like Johnny get the worst end of the stick, because unless you know them really well you couldn't know how unhappy children like him can be. Yet their behaviour denies them a lot of sympathy and loving which they need. He could be shouting at me one minute and hugging me the next. Oh, he had his troubles all right but as I say they're smoothed out now. His parents have separated you know – both of them are very nice, he sees them both and they are all good friends. I'm glad they are all being sensible about it, just as much for his sake as for their own.

'I'd often think when I accompanied Johnny that people used to judge him. I do wish people wouldn't come to judgments so easily. There is usually a reason for most things and a temper tantrum can't be pleasant for the person having it. I suppose if all of us on that bus had been as truthful about our feelings as Johnny a few more people might have been slinging some pretty ripe language around. As it was, at least he took their minds off just waiting for the next bus.

'Of course, as he got better he began to travel on his own and I was going to start with a new little boy when the ILEA decided to bring children like Johnny in by special bus with just two or three ladies looking after all of them as they were picked up. I suppose they saved money this way but I wondered if they considered before making the decision how far people like me and Mrs Nolan (another guide) had helped these children in our ordinary way?'

'I have always felt that was a bad decision, May, with regard to that particular handicap.'

'You agree with me then?'

'Yes.'

'Oh, I thought you might have thought I was being a bit cheeky.'

At this point she pressed a button on what looked like a brass or golden artichoke which was placed on a coffee table in her lounge. A Spanish toreador tune came from its heart and the leaves opened up to reveal a floral spray of cigarettes.

'How do you like that then?'

'I've never seen anything like it in all my life, May. Never!'

'Help yourself. Ernie bought it for me in Majorca.'

I took a cigarette, she lit it for me, pressed the button on the artichoke machine, and the sun sank over their Spanish holiday as the toreador song ended abruptly.

'I was talking about work wasn't I? It didn't take me long to find another job.

'I've done all kinds of work you know, some of it sheer drudgery. By that I don't mean just hard work, I mean boring work which gives you a pay packet but leaves you tired and empty. Now when I work with children, I'm tired all right, bloody exhausted some days, but the children, parents, teachers and different people that you meet just put that bit of cinnamon in the rice pudding' (she tapped her head) 'which makes all the difference to your life. I didn't want to give that bit of spice up so I got a job as a coach attendant, this time at a school for delicate children attending a special school in the East End.

'At first I thought it might be like being an over-attentive bus conductress but it isn't like that at all. You get to know all the children and lots of their parents too. It means an early start to the day, but Ernie is an early riser so that has never been no problem. Some of the children on my bus suffer from asthma attacks and some from epilepsy, it's a mixture of conditions which need that bit of extra attention. You see without having the experience of my son I wouldn't be half as much use as I am now as a person would I?' She answered her own question as I nodded agreement.

'Nor would I have made the friendships I've got with all kinds of different people I'd never have met. A handicapped child needn't make a lighthouse keeper of anybody. At least, I don't think so. It's done just the opposite for me. I feel I can go anywhere and talk to anybody whoever they are and just be me. Work is part of all this and I don't groan to myself before I leave the house in the morning and I've done that with some jobs.'

May paused for reflection. 'It was in the area of work that we came up against more problems with regard to Freddie.' She frowned, then changed her expression and said, 'I've got you a bit of salad and some nice ham, let's have it now with a cup of tea.' My welfare was suddenly her concern and we ate the salad and munched mince-pies as the Christmas tree in the corner blinked out intermittent seasonal good will to us and people passing on the pavement outside.

'In the last eighteen months or so Ernie and me began to wonder about Freddie's future in the working world. It's not all a joy-ride working for a living and nobody can expect otherwise, so the three of us, Ernie, me and Freddie, sat and talked over what Freddie might do when he left school. Do you know the school never contacted us about his work prospects. I did contact them and all they said was, "Oh, don't worry, Freddie will be all right."

'Well, in fact, I was worried because Freddie seemed to lose a lot of his fizz during his stay at the secondary school. He never complained about attending school, and I had no difficulties in that he attended willingly, but he was never enthusiastic about going like he used to be in the primary school. He became very quiet and I realise now that although he was well behaved he wasn't really happy and I have the feeling that he was left to stew quietly without anyone giving him the particular kind of attention and encouragement he needed.'

'Do you think he might have been better catered for in a special school, May?'

'If this school had been operating then, yes definitely, just the social side of it would have been marvellous for him, and a couple of years with Mr Jackson (careers teacher) would have done him the world of good. But to be honest, if I'd been offered the chance of a place at that time I would probably not have accepted it. Mainly because I would have thought he was being discriminated against. Now I know a bit more about it I see that discrimination would almost certainly have been in his favour. In a perfect world, I suppose there ought not to be children with handicaps. But it's not a perfect world is it? And those who are a bit less fortunate ought to help us others look more closely at ourselves because in helping them we are also helping one another.

'An all-age school would definitely have suited him better and I don't think that the older children at this school suffer in the way of relationships – most of them go to technical college as well and Freddie never had that chance. When I see your older children coming back as young men and women to say "hello", then I do feel that Freddie needed something like this. It's a kind of base for them isn't it? He wouldn't have become as "cut off" as he did at the big school, I'm sure of that.

'It was strange you know because we got Freddie his first job – it was in a watch-repair shop. I felt I could get a full-time job and heard that there were posts here for full-time women helpers. That was in 1969. I applied, I'd heard it was a new school and they gave me a time for an interview with the headmaster. The letter didn't give your name. I can remember waiting outside the room at the divisional office and when they called me down to go in for the interview you could have knocked me down with a feather. It was the shortest interview I've ever had. "Oh May", you said. The other fellow there looked a bit taken aback didn't he? I recognised you straight away, you looked a lot older than when I met you all those years before but your eyes haven't changed much. I remember you said that there was no real need for you to ask me any questions. Then you got up and instead of shaking hands we gave each other a peck on the cheek. It was a very good way of starting a new job together for both of us. Do you realise that was eight years ago, time goes very quickly.

'My Freddie's first job didn't suit him at all. It was at a

watch-makers, the pay was poor, and the particular routines there didn't suit him at all. We had very little guidance with regard to Freddie's career and we all eventually came to the conclusion that we ought best to seek for him what he would be the most contented in doing. This is easier said than done. We managed to find an apprenticeship in an electrical factory – but when the medical department knew of his past history of fits they turned him down. It made me very sad at the time, and I wondered whether or not I should have told them the truth. After all he hadn't had a fit since he was eight. I told the truth and that was that, my conscience was clear but I know with some employers I have come across that theirs can't be!'

May shrugged and said, 'It's time for a drink – sherry?'

I sipped. 'Is he happy now?'

'Oh yes, it's all worked out well and he works locally at . . . . He enjoys the job and he has some good mates there. He is football mad like the rest of them and he travels all over the place to watch the Arsenal play. To be honest Ernie and me don't see that much of him now.'

My eyes asked her the question and she answered without me having to say anything.

'Work, youth clubs, fishing and girls, they seem to take up most of his time. I'm glad because that's natural. There is one chasing him like mad at the moment.'

'What?'

May snorted. 'A girl!'

'Oh,' was all I said.

'He's twenty-two you know and we are all made the same but at that age it's the little differences that keep you going.' She chortled at her own expression and I gleefully accepted her worldly tolerance of the human condition. There was not much more to say, and she had ended the interview by persuading me to slosh back two more sherries in a short space of time.

'Here,' she said, 'we are going to Morocco next year. Can you imagine me on a camel?'

'Yes,' I said adamantly. If it were necessary that she should cross the Sahara or voyage to Trebizond then she would do it. As the situation stands I feel that the hazards and adventures that she had already undertaken take her well beyond the level of most forms of human endeavour and exploration.

Babs
Wilson

Fortescue Avenue runs directly off Mare Street, which is one of the main artery roads in the Borough of Hackney in London's East End. It is surrounded by small factories and is within 200 yards of a bingo hall and a cinema. The bingo hall is probably the more popular at the present moment. Pubs are numerous, but the New Lansdowne Working Men's Club with its large dance hall seems to be the biggest centre of attraction for the local settled working-class population. The land which this club now occupies was, up until 1913, a refuge for penitent females (discharged women prisoners). It functioned as a permanent memorial to the work of that lovely Quaker lady Elizabeth Fry who died in 1845. A plaque within the club still records this.

Fortescue Avenue is one of the few remaining streets in the area which give a further testament to the past. It is small and narrow. The Victorian bay windows stare across at one another separated by thin pavements and a 20-foot roadway. It is not an unattractive street, and in an area riddled with high-rise flats and demolition, it manages to pervade an atmosphere of stability in the seemingly endless areas of change which surround it. Many of the families have lived in the street for generations and many are inter-related. When Babs Wilson told me that it was under possible sentence of death from the local planning department the news shouldn't have surprised me, but nevertheless it registered a shock. The passing of the street will be a sad event. Kenny and Babs Wilson live at number 13, Kenny's sister lives at number 27, his mother at number 9, his mother's sister at number 3 – it would seem to be one of the few areas of instinctive family community areas left in London. It still retains a natural kind of order, similar to the construction of a cobweb, the needs of the family being almost totally met by the immediacy of their environment. Kenny and his brother are London taxi drivers.

'Oh there were only three of us in my family, we lived just off of Mare Street. I worked in a cutting section of a clothing factory when I left school. It was hard work as well. There were eight of us girls on our floor and I was the first one to have a boy friend. It was Kenny.' Babs Wilson smiled as she spoke and pushed the blonde curls and ringlets away from a face which is proof that some women can look beautiful at forty plus. The blonde hair frames a peaches-and-cream complexion which is enhanced by large grey-green eyes. The smile is unforced, warm and friendly.

'There was never anybody else but Kenny really; I think he knew it. He must have done, because all the girls on my floor had married before me, although I was the first one to be courting. He had a motorbike in them days and we had some good times. I can't remember him asking me to marry him. I think we just accepted it as the general run of things. Of course, Kenny wanted us to get married in a particular church which wasn't in the area where we was living, it was only just outside of it though. You know what Kenny's like – well, he went to see the vicar. The vicar said that some couples just gave an address that was in the parish boundaries and Kenny said, "You don't want me to begin my marriage with a lie do you?" He married us there without any more quibble, it was all natural-like, as I said, we seemed to know we would marry right from the beginning. We didn't have to talk about it.'

It proved a sound marriage; Kenny and Babs make a very complementary couple. The truthfulness of their relationship is very defined and it would be difficult to imagine them apart. However, it wasn't all bliss.

After two daughters, a son was born to them in the Mother's Hospital off Mare Street. They had waited and hoped a long time for Andrew's arrival. . . .

'It's a boy.'

According to Babs, Kenny immediately asked, 'Are they all right? I mean is my wife well and is my son all right?' Kenny, like most men who have experienced paternity, was confused as to whether or not he should laugh or cry with relief. He is not afraid to express his emotions, so one would imagine he did both. Babs and Kenny are a striking couple in that physically he is broad and stocky, swarthy-complexioned, handsomely featured, crowned with thick black hair, always well groomed with a trace of Brylcream. The contrasts in their physical appearance give them a distinctive romantic appeal even in their forties. I think they are aware of this – certainly on any social occasions both of them can cause the heads of opposite sexes to turn and take a second glance.

Babs returned home from the hospital with a small ticket containing the following information:

Date of birth, 2/7/64.   Weight, 7 lbs 13 ozs.   Sex, male.
Name, Wilson.   Delivery, normal.

In retrospect Babs does not query any of this information with the exception of the last detail: 'I know childbirth is not without some pain – after all, I'd had two children before Andy – but at one period not long after my labour had started, I had the most excruciating pain. It was so bad that I shrieked. I'm not sure they must have heard me across the Marshes. I asked about what had happened and I think it was caused during the internal exploration. Compared with the births of both my daughters, Andy's arrival was hardly normal. This is why Kenny particularly asked if Andrew was all right, because Carol my second child was born with a cleft palate and it is easier to accept and understand things if you are given some knowledge of them. So you can well understand Kenny's sense of urgency on Andy's behalf. When I arrived home with Andy with a clean slate from the hospital, you can imagine how happy we all were.'

The celebration was short-lived. Babs noticed that Andrew seemed a bit 'floppy'. She had been informed that there was slight toxaemia during the pregnancy, but had been reassured this had not affected Andrew in any adverse way. Nevertheless, at two months, during a periodic medical examination, it was mildly suggested that Andrew was not progressing as well as could be expected physically. At two years Andrew was referred to the Hospital for Sick Children at Great Ormond Street and there was subjected to many tests of a varying nature in order to come to some kind of conclusion as to the nature of his physical debilities and what might conceivably be the cause of them. This proved a very testing time for Babs, as Kenny probably externalised his concern and anxieties more than she did. Apart from these pressures, she already had two young daughters to care for, and organising the priorities of attention towards the individual children gave her some problems, as clearly a handicapped child would demand more time and special thought by definition. Fortunately the two daughters, Jackie and Carol, realised this and never seemed to resent the fact. The family discussed this together often and I am always moved by the consistent and corporate care that both daughters extend to their younger brother.

Babs and Kenny found the physical diagnosis easy to accept because it was apparent. They were informed that Andrew was suffering from a dorsi-lumbar scoliosis and that this would result in a curvature with regard to his stature. At this early age the degree of curvature did not seem too apparent. Even so the clarity of the condition gave them cause for deep sadness. Perhaps more worrying for them was the addendum on the report. This read quite simply 'in addition to scoliosis he appears mentally retarded'.

Both parents questioned the addendum and the hospital went through an exhaustive series of tests to see if the physical defects had in any way contributed towards the retardation. The conclusion remains still a very 'open verdict' and from a medical viewpoint it was termed as unexplained, but apparent. Brain damage was not suggested – an EEG test showed moderate diffuse abnormality, but this in itself might not cause any retardation whatsoever. It is the question marks that caused the stress and the difficulties of accepting what still remains a somewhat mysterious condition. Babs knew that on an educational level there would be difficulties with Andrew and it is in this area where she and Kenny combined together to defeat medical, and, to some extent, educational prognosis.

Before Andrew was due to commence schooling, they spent a great deal of time with him on social training, initiative undertaking and speech. In fact, I feel that all of the family must have provided him with intense pre-school training to equip him with the amount of independence he had acquired by the age of five. Nevertheless, it was felt both by medical and educational authorities that Andrew should attend a special school. Kenny fought this decision and the local authority accepted his views and agreed to Andrew being admitted to an ordinary infants' school if a sympathetic headmistress could be found. Of course, Babs found one.

I heard from this very kindly lady three years after Babs had found her. The telephone rang and the voice corresponded with the image that Babs gave me of her later.

'Oh, Mr Wakefield. This is Miss Herd here, Gayhurst Infants' School. It's not an inconvenient time to talk is it?'

'No, assembly is at a quarter to eleven.'

'I have a child here, one of my children, I think that you will be receiving his notes. His name is Andrew Wilson.'

'Yes, I have them. They arrived yesterday.'

'I hope you don't mind me telephoning, but I think communication means more than just reports and we are dearly fond of this child and his parents. I do feel for them both, particularly his mother.'

Miss Herd was not unusual with regard to headteachers of infant schools, who always showed a deep interest in children they felt needed another kind of education than that which they could provide. However, there was a gentleness about the voice which gave the telephone call more than its usual poignancy.

'They have refused special placement at one school and I know that father is somewhat resistant. I suggested that they visit your school and then decide. In all honesty there is little that we can do for their child here – we have helped him in all the more obvious social areas, but he will require very special help educationally. It might seem that the parents are being difficult, but I can assure you that is not the case.'

'I will contact the divisional office and arrange for an appointment; it is most kind of you to telephone.'

'Not at all, not at all, please do help them all you can. They are a most attractive couple and Mrs Wilson is a dear. You will let me know what transpires?'

'Yes, yes of course I will, I'll contact you after the interview. It has been good talking to you, perhaps we will meet sometime.'

'I am sure we will; I will wait to hear from you then. Good-bye.'

I marked the date for interview in my diary. One is always careful to digest notes and records before an interview and some-times one has an image of a child before he or she arrives. The image is usually wrong. In the case of Andrew, Miss Herd had somehow indelibly printed in my mind the first foetus of a family with which for one reason or another I knew that I would be inextricably involved for a long time. I read the notes after school had ended that same day, then left them to stew, not wishing to look or think about the sum total of their prognosis. Like a casserole, I hoped that the time lapse between my seeing the notes and having the interview would somehow improve the suggested and implied gloomy educational outlook for Andrew. Miss Herd had definitely contributed some savour as only a really good chef could.

I met Babs, Kenny and Andrew on 6 November 1970 at fifteen minutes past ten precisely. That sounds like a telephone time check, but reflects the kind of exactitude with which Babs seems to approach most things. She is unflurried, appears to be over-relaxed, sometimes to the point where she seems to be on another planet, yet this is a veneer which covers a steel-like will and a quality which no emergency can perturb.

I noticed that the parents didn't sit together. Babs chose to sit on one side of my room and Kenny sat on the other. Andrew stood at Kenny's side. Their positioning upset my sense of geography with regard to the interview. The huge desks which headteachers are provided with (i.e. to sit behind) have always seemed to me like the Great Barrier Reef at such times and I always tried to leave the position and join parents in what floor space was left around the small coffee table. There was only one chair left and a rocking horse. Andrew strayed from his father. I thought he would climb on to the rocking horse and moved to take up the one vacant chair. Andrew chose the chair and not wishing to encumber myself with permanent injury I left the horse jockey-less, nodded good morning, shook hands and returned back behind the Barrier Reef feeling slightly thwarted.

The notes and records of Andrew were on the desk before me. They were fulsome and varied – there were reports from teachers, headteachers, psychologists, doctors, health visitors and consultants. The final conclusion was that Andrew should be given a trial period in an ESN(m) school, but that he might probably prove to be ESN(s). I found it difficult to present the situation to them or to say that I was offering Andrew placement on 'trial'. However, I did say it, I expressed it badly, awkwardly, possibly because I couldn't stomach their reaction yet knew that I had to. I delivered the information quietly, but much too quickly. Usually, one can assuage parents in such situations with relevant diversions such as extra help on leaving and travel facilities to school, but from the look on Babs's face my 'comfort' verbiage dried like a drop of dew might if it hit the Sahara. I just said, 'Did you want to talk or ask me anything?'

'Kenny said we should stay in the taxi he had parked just outside the school. We had arrived early, about ten minutes to ten. We sat there in the cab, Kenny talking most of the time. He had worried a lot the night before going over this point and that, the way he always does. We had refused to accept a place offered in one school, we had heard of your place, we knew it was popular with parents and the infants' headteacher had said it was good, but over-subscribed. Kenny had decided that if we liked what we saw, we would get Andy in whatever happened. You know what a fighter he is, once he's got his teeth into something he won't let go.

'I liked the look of the building from the outside, it looked different, more like a small hotel than a school. I liked the gates and I noticed that the high wall around the playground had bricks with holes in them so that there was nothing "shut off" about the appearance like there is in some buildings. We left the cab a minute or so before the interview – but I remember seeing bright pictures on the walls of the hall and just in the entrance of the door was a list of everybody who worked in the building, teachers, speech therapists, the welfare lady, cooks, cleaners – I'd never seen that before. A boy had come to collect an envelope from your secretary and saw us looking. He said, "Hello, do you want Mr Wakefield, he is in there." Your door was open and Rosemary (the secretary) just paused in her doorway and said "Mr and Mrs Wilson? Mr Wakefield's expecting you, do go in." My first impression was that it was a friendly place, there has been no anxious waiting outside like it is when you visit a hospital.

'You were closing a drawer at the bottom of your desk, you popped your head up, smiled and said "hello" and asked us to sit down. Then you came round to us, shook hands and then went back behind the desk again. I knew the papers on your desk were Andy's. You didn't read them (I expect you already had), but you fingered them as you looked at us. I thought you looked young to be in such a job, but I remember thinking you looked tired. The telephone rang and you told the secretary to make a note of it and you would phone back. At least you were going to give us your time without interruption, then I thought you were "old-headed", it just means you think older than you are. You said something to Andy, but he didn't answer and it didn't seem to worry you, but then you worried us. You spoke quietly, but quickly and it took a few seconds to digest what you said before it finally sank in.

'Kenny leaned forward on his chair and straightened his tie a bit. You had asked us if we had anything to say. Well, Kenny had plenty didn't he?'

He did have plenty to say. He said it with anguish and urgency which I might have interpreted as being aggressive had not Babs been sitting there. Kenny was carried away by the force of his own arguments. This was hardly surprising as he was defending what was tantamount to a prognosis or judgment on his only son's future schooling. He disagreed and was stating very clearly his terms of reference for his beliefs. Babs didn't say much but she looked at me more than Kenny did who was concentrating more on what he had to say than on my reactions to his words.

Babs gazed at me throughout what at times almost amounted to a verbal tirade. Occasionally she would place a restraining hand on Kenny, who needed to talk, but never did she check him. If he made a salient point she would smile at me and nod approval. At one stage I intervened to point out the differences between an ESN(m) and an ESN(s) school. I might have saved my breath – both parents were fully aware. Babs took the issue further and said she could not accept that Andrew was subnormal. I expressed my sentiments on this issue and said I disagreed with the Ministry's category of educationally sub-normal. Kenny brightened at this and began to look a little more relaxed. It was Babs who spoke for a change. 'Oh, I'm glad you think that, it's not that Kenny and me think that Andy does not need a special school – he does, but to be truthful I don't see any kiddies as sub-normal.'

Kenny had expounded what Andrew could do. He could wash and dress himself. He could take messages within the immediacy of his environment. He could draw and he could build. He could and did help Kenny with his taxi. He could help about the house. He could be sent on errands to shops within the vicinity of his street. I couldn't dismiss these arguments and I admitted Andrew that morning. There was no distress at parting parents from child, Babs just saw Andy to the classroom door and her son dismissed her with a smile and a perfunctory wave. He did not appear to feel insecure about his parents leaving him.

Kenny shook hands and left for his taxi – I could hear the engine – and Babs was left alone with me for a very short time, mainly to sort out technical issues such as the times and place where Andy would be picked up by the school bus. She must have sensed that Kenny had not convinced me and that I had conveyed my doubts. She turned round as she was about to leave and looked at me compassionately.

'Kenny does get heated up sometimes, but he doesn't mean it hurtfully.'

Her head went to one side, she smiled and said, 'But he is right about Andy. He is right.'

They gave me a lift in their taxi as I had to attend a meeting that morning. Babs talked about Hackney, of how it had changed. When I got out of the cab she cautioned me about wrapping up warm. The raincoat I was wearing was ill suited to the freezing cold weather. With all her worries she had time for some concern for the welfare of a stranger. The gale-force winds and the driving rain made the tower blocks look possibly bleaker than they really were. I knew that Babs knew that I was not hopeful for Andy's future. I wonder how Andy would have fared at the top of a tower block. There must be other Andys dotted about the country much higher in the sky than can possibly be good for them.

'As far as London goes, we couldn't be placed better with regard to Andy – the small streets around here and the shops (which are only a couple of hundred yards away) are a kind of village. And we have got him acclimatised to the area. He knows the people in the shops and some of the other kiddies living round here, it's a very personal area and I'm sure as far as his own initiatives are concerned, it's made a heck of a difference with him regarding his socialising. I can't see how he could have coped if he had been born on a big estate – some of them are very awkwardly placed with regard to shops and amenities. Understanding neighbours are important and a boon and a blessing, but imagine what it might be like having one beneath you when you have a handicapped child. They can't all be helpful and some might be just the opposite. No, I can't complain about where we live, but I do feel for streets that are not so well placed as me.'

Babs knows that at some stage in the near future their 'village' is due for demolition. She has tried to get the dates when the clearance is due, but information is vague and the planning is going through the usual protracted sequences. In the meantime, it provides her with a long-term worry.

'We bought the caravan on Canvey Island with Andy in mind. It's not the most beautiful of places, but there is lots of space, plenty of grass, a kiddies' playground and the sea. It's no longer strange to him and it proves that once he is familiar with his surroundings, he can use them providing there is something there to use. You have seen him there yourself. He never gets lost or loses his sense of wonder about the place. I think for the future, when we have to leave here we must try to find somewhere similar – perhaps just outside of central London. I don't see how he could achieve the sense of community he needs on the newer estates. To be honest, I would find it difficult myself. I suppose Kenny and me would never have talked over so many things as we have if we hadn't had Andy. In this sense, I suppose Andy has brought us closer because Kenny has always wanted to be the one in charge. What did you call him in the pub on Canvey?'

'A chauvinist.'

'Yes, he only laughed didn't he? But he's changed a lot since Andy came along, as I say. We talk things over much more and it's not always a case of me just listening now. At one time, Kenny would never have wanted me to work, but he is quite happy with the present situation. To be fair to Kenny, he's always worked very hard, too hard I think sometimes. He takes things a bit steadier now, but at one time he was in a very stressful state, that was when Kenny was managing a fleet of taxis. He worked or seemed to work all hours of the day and night. Part of this was on behalf of Andy, as Kenny felt we needed to save more with regards to the future of Andy. If we were forced into the position of buying a house somewhere, then Kenny didn't want to be in a position whereby he couldn't choose carefully.

'In fact, he took on too much and thank God he is just working on his own now. I suppose it's inevitable that you worry in a situation like ours, but you have to organise the worry. Kenny does this much better now. Again Andy has helped us in this way in that having him with us has forced us to get our priorities straight. His arrival has made us much more interested in the education of our own children now, in fact all children. If you had told me five years ago that I would be a school governor now, I would have said "fish might fly". I know Kenny is quietly pleased about that too. I don't suppose you would have seen Kenny buying the *Guardian* either, but he gets it you know and always plods through the education bits.'

Most of the family relations live nearby. If they had all figured largely or contributed towards Andy's development I feel Babs would have mentioned them by name. She has rarely referred to any of them, so I assume their role has been either perfunctory or negligible. There is one exception – Iris – Kenny's eldest sister who couldn't be left out of any tapestry. I saw and heard Iris Adams before Babs had ever mentioned her. I suppose one could describe her as a kind of white version of Ella Fitzgerald, not quite so large, but most certainly tall. Her rendering of 'Won't you come home Bill Bailey' can often be heard in Fortescue Avenue if it is being given its peak rendering for the old folk at the Lansdowne.

'You don't have to ask Iris for help, she doles it out because it just seems part of her nature, she's Andy's godmother and we are well aware of it.'

I was always beguiled with the way the two older daughters gave up their time and attention to Andrew. Jacqueline the eldest is now married. When I discussed this issue of the relationships between her daughters and Andrew, Babs surprised me. She stared at me and looked most grave. 'If you're going to write about it, then you must write down it all as it is. Yes, both girls have been marvellous in supporting Kenny and me, but you see they needed attention too. Carol, my youngest daughter, seems not to have been affected by it all. But my Jacqueline, since she has been married . . . well.'

Babs sighed. 'We've had some heart-to-heart talks and probably been more truthful about our feelings than we were before. Jacqueline made it very plain that although she never showed it to us externally, on the inside she was often quite resentful about the extra attention Andy had received. She even found that her own resentment to the situation made her feel guilty, and it was something she didn't feel able to express. She is a sweet girl and I think that she must have suffered more than we are likely to know. Anyhow, I'm relieved that we have talked about it – she has her own family to be thinking of soon and in a way I am glad she told me because we can see now why some upsets that we have had in the past seemed much worse at the time than they really were. You do think – not think – Tom, -er, -er, -er, mm?'

'Analyse?'

'Yes, that's it, you do that much more, Kenny does it too much sometimes. I know that one of the biggest reliefs that we received was when you said Andy was no longer with you on trial.'

'Trial?'

'Trial, that's what you said, Tom, sounds terrible doesn't it? Mrs Krever (Andrew's teacher) worked hard with him and at one of the parents' meetings she told us that you wouldn't let him go. Then a few weeks later you told me yourself and Kenny and me celebrated. I remember saying to you that I would help in any way at school – I felt I wanted to do something to show my appreciation.'

Babs laughed then recollecting our discussion.

'Talk about quick off the mark, I had hardly said it before I was enlisted as a bus attendant. I hadn't worked for years and to be truthful, after a few weeks, I realised what I had missed. I can't imagine now what it would be like to be house-bound again. Working here at school has probably done as much for me as it has for Andy. It might sound silly, but a Mum is just taken for granted a lot of the time and it was a strange feeling to be openly valued. Of course, Kenny is still the boss of our household and he still has his say more than me, but I think he senses that inside of me I'm more independent than I ever was. He consults me more and I can understand him more. It's funny that you can live with a man half your life and then see things in him that you never noticed before. You love differently, you even get fond of the faults.'

I don't think that Babs had ever grown fond of her son's physical deformity, but as it had appeared to be static both she and Kenny had come to accept it and after the initial concerns and anguish it provided them with little stress. It did not hinder him in any form of play or games and he was growing into a wiry but sturdy strong boy. Babs was given about eighteen months of time to bask in a sense of security over Andrew's overall development. Shortly after this period, we all seemed to notice the limp at approximately the same time.

'He's dragging his left foot isn't he Tom? Vetty Krever has noticed it as well. I suppose we will have to go back to the hospital again will we?'

She knew the answer. An appointment was made and Andrew was taken to see his specialist at Great Ormond Street. The next day she reported back to me. She spoke up trying to keep a cheerful expression on her face.

'Andy has to wear a brace, all the time, for quite a long time. He's being specially fitted and measured for it. They say it will correct his posture and straighten it up a bit. Kenny has seen the man who is making it, he's very good mechanically and he will see it is adjusted right. It should be ready in about three weeks and we all have to get Andy used to the idea of wearing it. At the moment, he's quite keen on the idea, it's like a novelty to him. I suppose he'll feel different from the other children here, I wonder how they will take to him being in it?'

'I think they'll ask what it is for, and we'll tell them. After that, given three days, they won't pay much attention to it. Children often show a much more level-headed compassion than adults about things like this Babs.'

'Yes, I hadn't thought of that, I suppose you are right. I wonder what takes that away from some of them when they become grown-up? Perhaps it's something to do with inno-cence.'

In three weeks' time Andrew appeared at school encased in his brace, fitted to him like a great plastic giant clam. It extended from his chin to just beyond the base of his spine. The other children reacted as we had expected. Andrew did not regard his novelty as a joy for very long, but from home and school he was inculcated into the need for accepting it for some time. He bore it all most stoically and all of us witnessed the enormous resilience and courage that this child possessed. There were few outward demonstrations of the contraption causing Andrew any emotional instability. Certainly it clearly made physical demands on him in that he was much less active and by the end of some days at school was clearly deeply fatigued. Emotionally it was causing some disturbance, as he had sporadic bouts of bed-wetting throughout this period. The brace was worn practically all the time and both parents were diligent in seeing that all the hospital's instructions were carried out.

In the months that followed, Babs was confronted with more visits to the hospital for more adjustments to the brace than one would have thought necessary. In spite of the continued adjustments the brace began to cut even more deeply into the child's back. We noticed this at school and Andrew's consultant must have noticed it too because he called Babs and Kenny for an interview with him. Babs asked me to accompany them. I agreed. All of us, Andy's teacher, me, Kenny and Babs were stricken with a sense of deep foreboding. It was not declared, but Kenny's white face when he picked me up at home early on that Thursday morning said it all.

Whilst we waited at the hospital Kenny pampered the rest of us, fetching us two, three cups of tea, chocolate biscuits. I felt like saying 'just sit here Kenny and stop bobbing about', but Babs knew her husband better than I did. Throughout this rather tense waiting Kenny only referred to the interview once.

'I want you in with us, I want straight talking, they'll let you stay with us won't they?'

'OK yes, of course they'll let me stay.'

I wasn't sure, but in some matters over the years one can become pretty insistent. In this case, I didn't have to be as the consultant raised no objections to my being there. In medical terms he told us that the brace would have no long-term effects in correcting Andrew's posture and he concluded that the curvature was increasing. The alternative to this prognosis was major surgery of which no assurance could be given that it was always 100 per cent successful. Kenny seemed to have grasped the essentials of the discussion and asked if he, Babs and me could talk about the situation alone for a while. It was agreed that I would see the consultant afterwards.

Babs remained calm but Kenny's face was ashen.

'Does this mean what I think it means?' he asked.

'It means unless you agree to the operation, Andy will eventually be much more pronounced with regard to his physical condition.'

'Look, spell it out, does it mean he will be bent, bent right over?'

'More or less Kenny, yes, yes, it does mean that. I'm sorry.'

There was a short silence and Babs looked towards me, Kenny had turned away.

'Kenny doesn't like hospitals and he hates the idea of the knife, but I suppose if we have to . . .'

Kenny intervened brusquely. 'We ain't got any option have we? Are you going in to see him then, Tom?'

I didn't want to prolong the present waiting around. I nodded to Kenny, tapped the consultant's door and went in.

He informed me that he would operate on Andy at one of the local hospitals as he was a visiting consultant to quite a number. The parents would be informed of the arrangements within a month. I told him that the parents were in agreement and Babs and Kenny were called in and all the usual formalities were dealt with very swiftly. There were others waiting to see the consultant.

We collected Andy from the playroom, Babs took him by the hand and linked arms with me as we made our way out. Kenny had walked quickly on ahead of us and was in the driving seat of the cab when we got to the taxi. 'Back to school then?' he asked abruptly. Babs smiled wanly and nodded. Kenny turned and looked at us all, then bent forward and wept. Babs took Andy out of the cab, I dithered. If I had sat and cried a bit with him it might have helped, but I couldn't.

'We'll be back in ten minutes or so – see you in a bit.' I caught up with Babs and all we did was to buy a bag of crisps. We ate them up, returned to the cab and left for the East End of London as if Kenny hadn't cried. We were dropped off at school and all Babs said was, 'All right then Kenny?'

'I'll see you later,' he said and then drove away.

After a few days a letter arrived giving details of the time for Andy's admission to hospital. He was to be admitted to Hackney Hospital. This seemed a good idea to us as it meant that as it was in such close proximity to the school that we would be able to visit him daily and thus keep our contact with him. This way, from his point of view, his state of hospitalisation would be less traumatic. There would be no total severance from his home base or his schooling. In this sense, Andrew's pending admission was faced with bright optimism by all of us concerned with his future. 'Now we have decided it's much easier than I thought,' said Babs the evening before Andrew was due for admission. Andrew was prepared for it and as usual seemed to accept what was coming more stoically than most children.

The admission day arrived and I arranged to see Andrew after school – Babs took the morning off school in order to help her son acclimatise to his new surroundings. The situation passed from my mind, lost in the pressure which is always there each and every school day. My secretary found me in the housecraft room at 10.45 and said, 'Kenny is here Tom, he looks upset, he says he has to see you now.' Rose, our cookery teacher, nodded an understanding goodbye and I was met by Kenny who stood at the top of the steps leading into my room. I hadn't reached him before he began to talk.

'I've left the cab running, you'll have to come with me, I can't let him stay in that hospital. You must come and see for yourself. It won't do.'

I put on my coat without replying and he talked in the cab. 'Now you know as well as I know that nursing and care is as important as the operation, don't ya. Well you do, and this environment won't do for Andy and he's not staying.'

I tried to calm him, but it proved more provocative than assuaging.

'Well Kenny, if you have decided not to let him stay there, what do you want me for?'

'Because you should bloody well see it, that's why.'

I couldn't argue with it and didn't; besides Kenny was bigger than me.

He marched me quickly to the ward and Babs was sitting near an unmade bed. She sat with her head bowed, Andrew beside her unchanged. She looked up and for the first time I saw Babs crying, quietly, but the tears were there. Kenny's rage had left him speechless and so it was left for Babs to explain matters. She pointed at the bed. 'I'm supposed to get him ready for bed, but look at this linen, it's dirty – and look at the state of the lockers and what's this bag of dirty linen doing just dumped here?' I sniffed. 'Is that what the awful smell is?' I asked. 'No, it's there.' She pointed to some dead flowers which gave off a most unpleasant, fetid, rank smell. 'We don't feel confident, Tom, we can't leave Andy here. Kenny has complained to the Sister, but he's probably gone a bit too far; anyway she is busy at the moment.'

I looked at her causes for concern and there was no doubt that she had a just case for worry. I pondered as what to say for the best. I wasn't given much time for rumination.

'If Andy was your son, now try to imagine it Tom, if he was your son, would you let him stay here?'

Kenny gripped my shoulder and I could not be anything but truthful under such urgency. I reached for Andy's coat and said, 'No Kenny, I wouldn't, no I wouldn't, we will go back to school and see what other arrangements can be made.'

After some enquiries, we arranged for Andy to see another specialist at Great Portland Street. In the meantime, Babs wrote to the Hackney Hospital and received the following reply.

THE CITY AND EAST LONDON AREA HEALTH AUTHORITY
(TEACHING)

Telephone: Administrative Offices:
01-985 555.   Ref. TD/MB.   HACKNEY HOSPITAL,
                                             LONDON, E9 6BE.

Thursday,
16th May, 1974.

Dear Mrs. Wilson,
Thank you for your letter about your son's brief stay in Ward D.5, which was passed to me for attention.

I am sorry that this matter has taken so long to investigate; this is partly owing to the some two months which has elapsed between the events you describe and our receiving your complaint. Nonetheless, I have managed to obtain most of the necessary information.

Perhaps I may deal with your points, one by one.

I understand that there was dirty linen on the bed when you arrived. We sometimes have a problem with linen supplies, and this was no doubt exacerbated by the shortage of laundry staff which we were then experiencing. Nonetheless, there was no excuse for what happened, since the ward and laundry staff have instructions about what should be done if linen supplies run out. I apologise for what happened on this occasion. Your complaint has been helpful in giving us the opportunity to remind ward staff of their responsibilities.

I am sorry, too, that the flowers were faded, that the laundry bags had not at that time been removed and that the locker was not clean. As far as the screens are concerned, we have been unable to find out which screens were in use on February 25th. Certainly I understand that the ones in use at present do not fit your description. We have procedures for dealing with all these items and I am sorry that they were not followed, as they should have been in this instance – although we were, I understand, particularly short-staffed at the time.

I could perhaps mention that the major building work in progress in this area (which you will be glad to know, should eventually lead to greatly improved ward facilities and a much better general appearance) has made it particularly difficult to keep the whole D Block area as clean and tidy as we should like it to be.

This is, however, no excuse for some of the things you mention, but cannot have helped your general impression of the ward.

As you can see, your complaint has enabled us to attend to several of the matters you referred to in your letter. I am sorry that the service we provided was inadequate and hope that we have been able to put these various matters right for the future. Thank you for writing to us.

Yours sincerely,

Signed: Tim Davies
Acting Hackney Hospitals' Administrator.

Mrs. B. Wilson,
13 Fortescue Avenue,
Hackney, London, E.8.

Mr Ackroyd the new specialist clearly established a good rapport with Kenny. He explained in detail the delicate type of operation he was to perform on Andy and indicated that Andrew would be hospitalised for some months in Stanmore Hospital. I was pleased to hear this as I had visited this particular hospital before and on that occasion I was most impressed. Kenny and Babs made a preliminary visit and I arranged to visit with them on the second occasion. There were good reasons for this. In the first place, the hospital had invited me and wished to discuss Andrew with me (how encouraging this was), second, there was a school attached to the hospital and I wanted to see the headmistress and the staff to discuss Andrew's particular educational problems. This proved beneficial, as Andrew was to stay there for five months.

'The operations are complicated, but they have explained everything to Kenny and me and we are very impressed. That's not to say we are not anxious, but we have been given such complete information that we have nothing to quarrel about. We feel sure that they will do their best and we don't have the terrible fears of not knowing what is going to be done. Andy is going to have a bit of a tough time, but if we all support him, I'm sure he can get through it. Did you have a talk with the headmistress Tom?' Babs was calm and spoke with relief.

'Yes, I have arranged for a teacher at school (Ann Lea) to come over here once a week and I have seen some of the teachers who will be helping Andy after his operations. You know that he will be here for quite a long time Babs?'

35

'Yes, we've accepted that and one of us will get to him every day, it's quite a journey, but with facilities like this it's worth it. Kenny is so relieved about it all, have you seen the beautiful wards, and the playrooms? These grounds are lovely, just what the kiddies need when they are recovering. It's going to be difficult for Andy but I feel that they are all with us.'

The headmistress of the school, an honest, compassionate woman, emphasised this when she saw Babs and me together with other teachers who would later be helping Andy. He was given time to settle in to the hospital before the medical treatment and surgery commenced.

'Kenny has signed for the operation, it's tomorrow – he knows so much about it and this knowing everything has made him so much less agitated. Tomorrow he has the halo on, this is screwed in at the head, back and hips. Then after a while, he has to have it off and also a rod called the Harrington Rod has to be clipped somewhere in his back. This is the most difficult part, but we have to take it all as it comes. I'm confident, but I'm still doing some quiet praying.'

Babs stayed at the hospital the next day whilst the halo was assembled. I arranged to see Andy with both parents the following evening.

'Oh, Tom, Andy made me blush yesterday, the halo is on, but he doesn't like it, but he knows now he has to live with it for a while. When it finally dawned on him that he must put up with it, he came out with such a torrent of swearing. At first, I thought to check him a bit, but then I thought it best to let him rip for a while and get his feelings off his chest. What is good for his Dad would be good enough for him. I reasoned it that way. It seems to have worked because he's calm enough now. Wait till you see the poor soul, he looks like something from outer space. I don't think he is going to be quite so interested in *Dr Who* after this is all over.'

I went with Babs and Kenny and Andy was receiving excellent attention from all the staff. He said he wanted to tell me a secret, so with permission from Kenny and Babs I let him whisper. 'Mr Wakefield,' he cupped his hand behind my ear and waved his other hand to indicate that he wanted Babs further away so that she could not hear what was to be said.

'Mr Wakefield, here, can you tell them to get this off me?'

'No Andy I can't.'

'You're in charge, you can.'

'No I'm not in charge, we all agreed that you must put up with it, you know why. You have to help us. I think you're very brave and I'm going to tell John Donnelly at school that you are braver than John Wayne even.'

'Will I be able to ride a horse then?'

'Yes, later if you help us.'

'OK then, but tell John Donnelly' (Andrew's friend at school) 'don't forget to tell him.'

It would be over-optimistic to say everything went according to pattern – there was the frightening period after the op·ra- tion when the clip dislodged. The process was repeated and th.s proved a blessing as the curvature was decreased even more and the operation was totally successful. After five months Andrew was back with us at school and within seven months he could join in all physical activities. Babs watched him dancing in the hall.

'Oh, isn't he naughty, he won't stick to his partner, he does tease John Donnelly.' She smiled and said, 'His back is straight, I don't have to think about scoliosis any more. I'm so grateful, I can't tell you how good the feeling is.'

'How do you feel about the special school situation now Babs?'

She looked at me knowingly.

'Well, I know more about it and that helps, and all schools vary don't they?' I let her continue. 'I suppose if the world were perfect there would be no children with handicaps and if all schools were perfect then they could be designed, equipped and staffed to cope with all kiddies. But I know the world's not perfect, and certainly I don't see how all schools can be. Andy couldn't have got through all of this without special schooling. Yet in a way, it's special people that count for more.'

'You're one of them,' I said.

'Yes, yes, I suppose I am, I'd never thought of it that way. I have a lot to thank my Andy for – just look at him Tom. Just look at him. He has got a future.'

Rose
Seward

As early as just twenty years ago the first glimmers of concern were expressed on behalf of 'non-communicating children'. In some cases these are children who make little or slender attempts to communicate, even by gesture. Some have speech, some a little speech, and others none at all. Their world does not appear to extend much beyond wishing to be left alone with their own habits and obsessions. Sharing is a most difficult process which most of them appear to find painful. Perhaps it might have been simpler for parents, doctors and teachers if any physical damage had been diagnosed with such children, as an injury of one kind or another is easier to accept. The blame for behaviour is sweetly placed on the aftermath of the affliction. I know of no handicap that places more stress on a parent or a family than the child that we have come to view as autistic.

'If somebody else might benefit from hearing about my son Michael then my God I'll talk because I wouldn't want anyone to go through what I have gone through. When I look back I don't know how I've survived it all.' Rose Seward smiled wryly. It would seem that the smile, coupled with an irrepressible amount of sad realism, must have been two of the major factors contributing to her survival. She smiles easily and when she laughs the laughter takes over her whole frame and becomes contagious. Her pale blue eyes and sense of fun did not go unnoticed by her husband.

'I met John at work, hardly a glamorous place to meet, is it?

I mean he never asked me to dance at the Hammersmith Palais
or anything like that. He was a wood machinist and I was a
shorthand typist and we "noticed" each other in the canteen.
That sounds cut and dried but it was romantic and it still is.
We began courting and he did Army service in between and
when this was completed we married. We had known one
another for four years by this time and 1950 will always be a
special year for me. We had found a flat to go into – oh, you
should have seen that place. It was in Blackfriars, Southwark,
and it was known as a tenement flat. There are still a few of
them around. There were just two rooms, no bathroom and a
loo outside on the landing. I have no grumbles because we had
the flat to ourselves. We made a little picture of that place, it's
like that when you have your first home. The old girl opposite
said to me, "Oh my word Rose, I can't recognise it."

'We waited a while before we decided to start a family, in fact
it was six years before I was pregnant, it was all planned and I
very much wanted a baby. John and me felt that this would
make our lives even more complete.' Rose rubbed her chin,
looked away from me and then gazed back. Again the sad smile.
'Oh, dear God, what we got for a moment of pleasure.'

The moment of pleasure extended itself into happy content-
ment throughout the pregnancy. 'I enjoyed all of it, I felt fine
and worked right up to the six weeks before the baby was due.
It was an exciting time and I looked forward to the big event
like a child does waiting for Santa Claus. The preparations were
fun too, getting a cot, nappies, and watching my mother knitting
frantically. Yes, we were all ready to celebrate. But it wasn't
like waiting for Christmas. The twenty-fifth of December is
Christmas and that is that. I had to wait twelve days over the
expected time of delivery before I was finally admitted in the
General Lying-in Hospital (now St Thomas's) in York Road.
The labour pains began at 7 a.m. on the Tuesday morning, and
I know this might sound difficult for you to believe, they went
on and on until mid-day the following Friday. My husband
visited intermittently and has since said that I was hardly conscious for most of the time. My own feelings about it are that I
was too busy concentrating on the birth itself so that I wasn't
able to take too much notice of visitors. I know that I felt I had
reached the ultimate in exhaustion but you see, in a way, I was

so innocent. It being my first baby I was unaware that my situation was any different than any other would-be mum's. I felt that what I was going through was just the usual process. I know I moaned a lot, I had to, and after what seemed like the whole of my lifetime my little boy was born. It was a "normal" delivery. The delivery might have been but what went on before and what happened immediately afterwards was far from normal. I was allowed only a momentary glance at my son before they whisked him away to an incubator – he looked like a piece of wrinkled paper. I remember thinking, he's mine, he's mine. I was given a hot-water bottle and then I had the sweetest and most welcome sleep of my life. I've never slept like it since.'

It might be as well to consider the effects of Rose's experience on all three people involved, that is Rose herself, her husband and the baby. Rose had undergone the heaviest physical and emotional strain within her life-span and in spite of the 'sweet sleep' was still somewhat bewildered on recovery. Her husband had maintained his equilibrium in spite of experiencing severe anxiety on behalf of his wife and his baby. All he had been able to do throughout this period was to visit and reassure; if he had conveyed his personal agony and anxiety to his wife then he would have failed her. The baby was in no way physically injured but his birth was more protracted and more shocking than that of most babies. It was a traumatic birth but he had survived. All three people were affected and their future lives were all heavily influenced by the event.

'After four days they placed my baby in a cot, just near me. I was so pleased to have him there. My husband had known that the shock of the birth had put my child's life in danger. He had been given strict instructions not to say anything about this to me. He carried this knowledge for a month before he told me. All the strain, all the stress he kept from me. I don't care who knows it, I've loved my husband passionately since that time.' Rose paused, I thought she might be searching for another word, but she nodded her head. 'Yes, passionately, and I know that I always will. It might sound corny but it's true.'

Mystery still surrounds the underlying causes of what is now termed as childhood autism, and the factors behind these causes still appear strange and varied. The prospect of finding the causes sadly appears to be as distant as ever. In 1943 Professor

Leo Kanner first described such children in a special group – yet most workers with the autistic affirm that each child has different individual problems. These problems manifest themselves in certain behaviour disorders which need constant appraisal and attention if the child is going to be helped in any way at all. It does seem certain that autism is a condition which begins in infancy or very early childhood and there are some aspects of behaviour pattern which appear fairly common to most of these children.

What Rose Seward has to say is special to her but past mums will have experienced what she has undergone and so will many more mums in the future.

'I was so pleased to get Michael home, I didn't mind the sleepless nights for a week or so, but they went on and on and on. . . . He never stopped crying for three whole months; he'd sleep a bit, just fitfully, then the crying would start again. I cuddled him, sang to him, you name it and I did it. It was hell trying to feed him because he inevitably rejected his bottle. After two months I felt as much in a state of shock as my baby did. Don't forget I was used to being in an office and suddenly finding that my whole life was now domestically timetabled every minute of the day left me feeling as though I had been shipwrecked. John was marvellous throughout this period. When he got in from work he would take his turn with Michael as well. Just when I felt the endless crying was beyond me and that I couldn't cope with it for much more than another week it stopped.' Rose snapped her finger. 'Just like that. No rhyme nor reason, he just stopped.

'Michael was like a different baby, he lay quietly in his cot and I felt that he had just settled down.' Rose thought for a while and rubbed her forehead, her voice came out almost as a whisper. 'He went dead silent, placid almost to the point where one couldn't imagine him there if you had not been able to see him. I felt that he was void of any emotions – if there was anything going on in his little head he never expressed it. I was nagged with worry by this behaviour but hoped it would just be a passing phase – but after seven months he wouldn't hold things, anything, nor would he make any attempts to sit up. He just continued to lie there, that's all, he just lay there.

'It came as no shock to me when the local clinic suggested I attend Great Ormond Street hospital with my child. I had accepted the fact that there was something wrong and to be honest I was joyful about the prospect of going to the hospital.' Rose grunted. 'Looking back, I suppose I expected them to wave a magic wand and everything would be fine. There was no magic. They diagnosed brain damage but could not specify the type it was. I agreed to take Michael for a check-up each month. I did this, but there was no treatment offered, merely what seemed to be the same kind of examination each month. I never felt that anything was achieved by this routine and ritual except the fact that the fares to and from the hospital was an expense I could ill afford at the time. I suppose the brain damage diagnosis was at least something I could accept but it didn't give me much enlightenment on how I could help Michael. Quite honestly I felt that the professional people seeing Michael at the time were probably as bewildered as I was about him.'

Rose's conjectures are probably true, as there are differences of opinions and a variation of theories as to what causes childhood autism. Two main theories are being looked at and investigated at present One theory suggests that a physical or organic cause is the most likely. 'Brain damage' is still a very generalised formula that covers a plateau of medicine which is still very much at the explorative stage. However, it would seem that more and more people find this theory (with all its attendant question marks) more palatable and acceptable than the second main theory. Rose Seward rejects the second theory, along with many other parents in her situation, and looking at it purely from her point of view and gleaning what I can from her experience, so do I. Many parents, like Rose, find the other theory too painful to accept. This is not surprising as it places a great burden of anxiety on them. This theory, put very simply, adheres to the belief that autistic children are normal when they are born but that their nurturing and early environment bring about severe and lasting emotional disturbance resulting in autism. On the other hand, improper housing facilities do often cause terror and hazard for the mother of a handicapped child.

'Just before Michael had his first birthday an incident that might sound like a music-hall joke killed all the charms that my little tenement flat might have previously held for me. I had got up early as I liked to have breakfast with my husband before he left for work. We savoured these mornings as I could sit with my husband whilst Michael slept and it was always a peaceful time. I was still in my night-dress when John left that morning and I suppose I was still a bit drowsy, in spite of the tea I had drunk. In any event, I toddled off to the loo outside on the landing quite happily. There was no sense of happiness or physical relief when I returned, I can tell you. I had forgotten to bring my flat door-key with me. It might sound funny, me standing locked out in my night-dress but in reality I was filled with fright as I was afraid that Michael might wake up and find himself alone.' Rose shook her head and sighed.

'Well, I rushed to the flat underneath and borrowed a top-coat and some bus fare from the lady and went immediately, just as I was in my slippers and night-dress, to my husband's work-place for his keys. I got some funny looks from people on the bus but I couldn't think of anything but my baby. John gave me his keys and when I got back I found Michael still sleeping. You can't imagine the relief I felt to find him there. The forty-minute journey might have given some people travelling to work a morning laugh or joke seeing me as I was – but for me the whole episode was a piece of purgatory that I will never forget. "At this stage, Mrs Seward, your son ought to be able to discriminate between a knife and fork." Dear God in Heaven he's got all his life to learn to discriminate the difference between a knife and fork. I don't care if he chooses to eat with a damned spoon – but I do care as to why he is making no sounds, and I do care that for a lot of the time he seems as though he is on another planet and not on this world with me. What's the use of telling me something that I know already, help me to understand what I don't know.' At this stage, Rose probably knew more about her own son than any outside agencies; furthermore she persisted in helping him where other agencies which could be labelled 'objective' might well have failed.

'A child like my Michael was more expensive to rear. You see, when he became mobile he never crawled, he just dragged himself along on his bottom. It still astonishes me how he lugged himself around.' Rose laughed. 'I know endless pairs of trousers bit the dust, I always think of Michael's early childhood when I hear that phrase in cowboy films. Again, the next leap of faith came as a surprise or a shock, call it what you like, but on a Christmas morning at eleven he rose from his bottom. He stood, and then he walked. What a Christmas present! Poor lad, he never comprehended why my husband and me entered that Christmas spirit with such fervour. Yet to this day my Michael has never ever crawled. Strange, isn't it?'

Autistic children are often baffling in this way and over the years their 'strange' behaviour patterns have come to be termed as bizarre. Yet it would be as well to remember that though there may be what appear to be symptoms that are similar to many autistic children, each individual is often very different from other children that come under the same terminology or diagnosis. Autism in babyhood seems to manifest itself in either of two ways: (a) they scream and wail during the day and often long into the night, or (b) they lie placid and unresponsive to stimuli – even food offers no wonder or fascination for them. Rose's son clearly displayed both these symptoms and Rose found both equally stressful and worrying.

'I found out other strange things about him too – in a way it was just like exploring a new town. If you found a blind alley, then you just started in another direction, except that there was no *A to Z* to help me at the time. Do you know I knew that he could read even before he started at school? No one would believe me as he had never uttered a syllable, but I knew because I had discovered that he had a fascination for words and that he could discriminate between different shapes. I used to sing to him a lot (he loved hymns) and I talked to him. I would point to words in picture books and he would respond with a smile. I bought plastic letters from Woolworths, and cut them out of the paper and he would make words with them for hours on end. He could get the alphabet in its correct sequence in minutes and jig-saw puzzles enthralled him. He never seemed to have any problem in getting the pictures completed. The clinic probably felt that I was being defensive on my son's behalf but I always knew that he was not dull. Even so, I was relieved when he was referred to an ESN(m) special school at five; he entered that building mute. I did not complain because he obviously needed special education of one kind or another and the referral was useful in that after two terms the school confirmed my statements and agreed that he could read, that he

45

was not dull and that he was mis-placed. His education still posed a problem both for me and the education authorities. A kind of compromise was recommended. He attended a special unit for four days a week and a physically handicapped school for the rest of the time. The unit seemed to suit him more than the school. He was always happy to attend it, whereas the school held fears for him as he was loath to attend it and displayed this in different ways. One education psychologist put a theory forward that he might be aphasic as he did wonderfully well when tested, in fact he did everything except speak. Oh God, a child who poses mysteries as Michael did would put you off any detective novel for life.'

'Oddly enough, two months after this, we found a new flat. In fact it was half a house. It was an old house in Clapton, but we weren't going to quibble about its age. Six rooms all to ourselves was like moving to Buckingham Palace after what we had been used to. It was bloody marvellous, it meant John would no longer have to risk breaking his ankle by climbing over our bed in order to close the wardrobe door each night. You can only appreciate space when you have been without it.'

The new home gave Rose more security with regard to her environment and heralded some hope for the future as far as her son's development was concerned. Probably the most important research available with children suffering from debilities that are extraordinary is the detailed and careful information that caring parents like Rose can give. Mothers like Rose Seward who keep such records are well aware that they might in some way help other mothers who may also experience the anguish, despair and guilt that so often accompany the heavy responsibilities and committal thrust upon them on the realisation that they have borne a child who is handicapped.

'We had only been in the place a week or so when Michael sat up unaided. He was now thirteen months old, you know things like that become of importance when you are looking for chinks of light or hope. Any positive development stays like a tattoo on your heart. If I hadn't kept hoping then I don't think I would have coped – no I wouldn't have. Michael seemed to be constantly prone to minor illnesses like chills and colds, and visits to the doctor with him through all this became part of my domestic routine. All the usual development patterns that babies experience seemed to come late to my Michael. Either they came late – or they didn't come at all. I continued the routine check-up visits to the clinic. I can remember getting very angry when they confirmed my worst fears that there was something desperately wrong with him. It wasn't the confirmation that made me angry (I'm no fool, I'd guessed as much myself), it was the way they put it or chose to illustrate it.

A good detective should come up with surprises. An element of the bizarre is often present and with respect to parallelling her son's progress Rose's descriptions are sad but often exciting. At first I thought it was the heat that caused Rose to close her eyes momentarily. 'Would you like me to open a window?' I asked.

'No, I was thinking of Miss Henderson who ran the unit, an angel of a woman she was. She was there when Michael first spoke. I was there too, he was seven years old by this time. Each time I took him to the unit I went through a little ritual with him, sometimes he smiled so I always assumed that he enjoyed it. It went like this. I put his dinner money in his hand. I pointed to it and said, "Dinner Money", "Dinner Money". He would smile sometimes but sometimes there would be no response. "What's it for Michael?" Sometimes he would smile, again sometimes no response. However, on this particular morning he began to shake and quiver. Not just his head but his whole body seemed full of tremors, and then it came out. It wasn't loud but it was distinct and audible. D-i-n-n-e-r M-o-n-e-y. When he found his speech I lost mine. Miss Henderson remained calm and cool but I had to creep into her room. I just sat there and cried.

'After this I would try to conjure up all kinds of ways to get him to expand his speech a little. In the evenings, if we were doing a jig-saw puzzle, I would joke with him in a positive way – "Where's the missing piece, Michael, where the heck is it? We'll find it, we'll find it like we did your voice." He would smile when I went on like this but he didn't speak although I was in no doubt that he understood what I was getting at. Oddly enough, the second time he spoke there were other people present as well.

'Friends in a situation like mine are very important. Relatives had expressed sympathy but that was as far as it ever got.

47

I don't think any of them helped constructively, but if I am really truthful what could they have done anyway? It's only people who have experienced similar issues themselves or are steeped in working with such children who could possibly begin to comprehend all the hazards involved. I was visiting a friend – she also has a handicapped child – for tea. We were nattering together – and to this day I'll never know what prompted her to do it – when she half casually muttered to Michael, "Do you want orange juice or water Michael?" He said, "Water."

'Well, she nearly dropped the glass with shock and I took a quick gulp of tea to make sure I wasn't dreaming. But it had happened. He was beginning to speak. Really in much the same way as he had walked, with no gradual build-up. When progress comes this way it does seem truly miraculous. It makes you wonder how easily we accept all these developmental faculties when they come normally. I suppose it's only when they don't come that you can realise their real value. Other words followed, some of them completely out of context. I never understood why Michael announced "South Africa" one Sunday afternoon, nor did my husband, but to this day he is fascinated by maps.

'At eleven-plus Michael was confronted with a double change within the space of a year. The house we were living in came up for demolition. There was no denying it was in a bad condition, in fact if it had been left much longer as it was it would probably have fallen or caved in on us, so we were moved to a brand new flat. You've seen it. The flat itself is lovely but I would be lying if I said I enjoy it more than the old house because I don't. A high-rise estate is a bit like living on an ant-hill except that ants communicate a bit more. It's noisier than my other place yet the surroundings are not as friendly. I really do miss my other place and think I always will.

'In the same year Michael attended a secondary school for physically handicapped children. The staff tried very hard with him and the headmaster was a kind and sympathetic man. It was difficult to get Michael to go to school. I felt it held real and terrible fears for him. The headmaster agreed with me and confirmed that he felt that Michael was wrongly placed. Michael confirmed this opinion himself by developing alopecia. He looked a sorry sight with great tufts of hair falling from his head. Those bald patches were a testament to his worries, I know that.

'I had a series of talks with a friendly man called Dr Graham who eventually suggested boarding placement. I talked this over with my husband and after days of discussion we finally felt we ought to give the idea a try. We talked it over with Michael, who much to our amazement did not seem at all unhappy with the idea. We were given an address of an autistic boarding school and the appointment was made for interview. It was a marvellous place, we stayed all afternoon. After the interview we went to talk with other members of the staff. Michael promptly returned to the headteacher's room, looked the doctor straight in the eyes and said, "Please accept me for your school." They did. (The headmistress told me this some time after the first term had started.) He had virtually admitted himself, there was not an ounce of trouble getting him to go and his alopecia disappeared as his fears of his schooling subsided. He was happy and John and I were content for the time being.'

Rose's account of her severance from her son sounds a bland and easy procedure. It was only on closer questioning and enquiry that I realised that Michael had not just agreed at the snap of a finger to enter a boarding-school situation. He had in fact been well prepared by his mother who intuitively used the background of her own childhood and conveyed the happiness that she had experienced during the period of war-time evacuation. Her memories of this two-year boarding-school period were pleasant ones and she assured Michael that he would be home every weekend. There is no doubt that Michael was really looking forward to going away from home. The prospect of a boarding school held no dread for him; on the contrary, he had come to view it as a deserved pleasure. How many mothers of children without debility prepare their children for the first day of school? The first day of entrance in many schools can be quite traumatic. Schools are often criticised for this effect but not all parents can be abrogated from blame. 'You wait till you get to school, my girl, there'll be no sulking then, it'll be a clip around the ear and no questions asked.' I would hope this comment – which is not untypical of many parents – is, again hopefully, a total untruth for all schools in Britain or anywhere else for that matter. The most interesting facet of Michael's admission is that he opted for it himself. How many children attending ordinary schools would attend if they were not bound by social or legal compulsion?

For the first time since the birth of her child Rose was now free for three days each week to do with her time as she chose. She chose to work. My own school secretary had to enter hospital for five weeks. I was feeling a little forlorn and bereft as the intricacies of such a post are far more than anyone not involved with it could ever imagine. Rose was sent to me as a temporary secretary during this period whilst my permanent secretary (who had been with me for five years) was absent. Rose had no previous experience of the job. The job held worries for her but she managed them with a smile and what is more important she made lasting friendships with other parents and helpers whilst she was with us in the school.

It was only after a fortnight or so that I first heard of her son. She invited me home one Friday to meet him and I accepted. The first things I noticed in the flat was the carpeting. I had reasons for this as Rose had mentioned some of her son's past obsessive behaviour which had caused her alarm and also in-dented many of her plans for saving money.

'Oh, he had lots of odd, quirky habits, when one disappeared another one came. We all concentrated on diverting him away from them. Of course I couldn't help worrying about them but gradually I accepted them and then tried to do something about it. Fluff was the worst.'

'Fluff?'

'Yes, fluff, and bits of fluffy wool or anything like that, Michael saw or seemed to be enthralled by it. So much so that wherever and whenever he could find it, he would pick at it and eat it. It sounds innocuous, doesn't it, but it had me close to being a nervous wreck at times. I'll give you some examples, they might sound a bit funny now, you have to laugh in the telling of them, either that or you would cry and I have done enough crying over the years.

'One day I was accompanying Michael on a trip to Great Ormond Street Hospital, the bus was crowded but to my relief there was one vacant seat. My relief turned to horror as I sat down with Michael perched awkwardly on my lap. Sitting right in front of us was a large lady who was wearing the biggest angora wool cardigan that I have ever seen. I watched his eyes light up with fascination even before I could get my fare ready. Even before I could begin an attempt to divert his attention he had already tugged at the cardigan. The woman wearing it turned around and glared at me. There were a few more tugs after the first and I could sense the poor woman's irritation and anger. We had only to travel a couple more stops; it is just as well or the woman wouldn't have had a cardigan left. No, in all probability I would just have to have got off the bus and walked. How would you like to try explaining autistic behaviour on the top of a crowded number 38 bus?

'I have explained it, though; once when I took him on a boat trip from Westminster Pier to Richmond the same situation arose. There was no escaping this time, the boat was full and it is quite a long journey. I apologised to the lady and briefly tried to give her an idea of Michael's problems. She was very good about it all. She said she quite understood, and to make her point she did not move from her seat and even joined in with me picking out landmarks along the river and cajoling Michael into interest. You see you remember people like that, ones that show understanding and sympathy. Another time I accompanied Michael to a cinema with a friend and her little boy. Her son complained that Michael was eating his pullover! She didn't mind. I can laugh now when I think of it because he doesn't do it any more. Yet during the whole of that particular period when the obsession was rampant I was in constant fear and anxiety in case he should provoke someone who would interpret his actions wrongly. I was afraid that someone might strike him or attack him.' Rose's carpeting throughout the flat was nylon; it did not match the previous Axminster covering in quality but it carried no fluff. Its more expensive predecessor had been pulled and damaged by her son, so that huge bare patches created islands of destruction.

'We just had to get rid of the carpeting, we were also worried that Michael might get a hair-ball in his stomach, you know, in much the same way as cats do. Thank God that is past now, he doesn't do it any more.' Rose sighed and added that Michael still banged his left hand on his right. This has caused a deformation of his fingers which in turn impedes his typing. He can now type faster than he can write and knows the key-board well. This skill is encouraged both at home and at his present school.

'It's no good, I am not going to paint a rose-garden for anyone and I must tell you in all honesty that any thought of having another child after Michael was totally beyond me. Without birth control I would have found it all impossible to cope with. My marriage could not have survived it and neither could I. I would have been in a perpetual state of fear and I feel that the reality of another pregnancy would have just finished me off one way or another. As it is, I know my health has been affected. The constant anxiety and nervous tension leaves me in troughs of depression from time to time and I'm sure it is my emotional state which gives me these endless throat infections. I have felt so exhausted at times that it feels as though I have run a hundred miles. Yes, it is a bit like a hurdle race.' Rose paused and ruminated for a few seconds.

'Yes, it's just like that, you scramble over one fence only to be confronted by the next. If you're not confronted by a problem then you begin to wonder. It's a bit like running in the dark.'

'I don't know quite what you mean Rose?'

'Well, nobody had told me what was wrong with Michael until he was nearly fourteen. Oh, they had said he was handicapped but this was already patent to me. There were all kinds of conjectures mooted around but no real conclusions. Then finally I was told – he is autistic. In a way I was relieved to hear it.'

'You mean you didn't mind him being labelled?'

'Well, there is a name for everything and it did give me a starting-point for treatment and the right place for him to be. I did feel a lot less bewildered about it all.'

It would be harsh to lay blame on the educational authority for the seemingly slow evaluation of Michael's condition. Diagnosis and assessment of his condition and needs could not have been arrived at quickly. Rose confirms this and makes it quite clear that the particular authority has been most generous in its provision and help. Michael's main initial symptom of retardation or disturbance was very slow development. If this alone had only been taken into consideration he would have probably been placed in an ESN (severe) school by the time he was seven. As it was all kinds of variation of placement were tried and clearly needed to be tried. In the event, no one had wrongly concluded that he was simply innately dull.

I suspect that parental pressure helped the number of 'try-out' situations that were provided for Michael. Given the complexities of his condition any one of them might have had some measure of success in helping him. The unit obviously did help him and two of the other special schools were instrumental in getting more assessment and diagnosis from a wide-ranging team. It also gave other people apart from Rose the chance to witness the islands of intelligence which her son possessed. This is probably the most important point to be gleaned in this form of debility, namely that prolonged and detailed observation by all concerned with the child's welfare is utilised in any way possible to produce results. Here again an autistic child will often confound the experts or the people closest to him. Progress often seems extraordinarily dramatic or spontaneous, but it would be niggardly to put such progress as is made all down to chance. Michael's speech, when it did eventually arrive, owed a great deal to the routines and rituals that his mother had presented him with. If he had never been subjected to any stimuli, either at home or at school, could one have ever expected any kind of responses or reactions? Or would he have withdrawn from the world completely? Obviously a complete opting-out from his environment would have been less painful at the time than the tentative steps of opting in. But it is clear that his present measure of contact with the world gives him pleasure; the initial fears, once overcome, are replaced by an increased awareness which must be continually strengthened. Educational placement of children like Michael will always be difficult and individual. For some a unit attached to a special school, for some a unit apart, for some dual attendance at two centres of learning, for some a boarding unit. There are some who argue fiercely against the formation of residential units, mainly on the grounds that it prevents school and home working together. This has not been so in Rose's case. The education of autistic children is still very much in the explorative stage and any blanket decision as to the kind of provision needed would be unproved and insensitive. Wherever such a child is placed psychiatric supervision should be available and the threads which bind parent, school and child together must be spun of the strongest materials available. In short, no amount of professional expertise will help without an enormous amount of sustained love and empathy. Rose puts this succinctly and the phrase that reiterates is 'I just want what is best for Michael'. Wanting what is best for her son is still causing her personal anguish and worry.

'At eighteen the educational authority are no longer obliged to take on the responsibility for a boy like my Michael. I was informed by the headmistress of Michael's boarding school that I should contact my local Social Services Department without delay. She had good reason for giving me this advice. Michael was continuing to make very good progress at school and she felt an extra year would be beneficial to him. As I had seen him every weekend throughout this last year I had no reason to disagree with her. He had become much more communicative and this was noticeable during the holiday periods which he always spends with us. He talked more often, in fact he even mentioned what his private world was like.

' "My world is all bare. It is all dark. It has no trees. It has no television. It has no work, no people."

' "I don't like the sound of that too much, Michael, no jig-saw puzzles, no records, no music. I think you had better come into my world more, join Dad and me. Do you want to join our world?"

' "Yes, mum. Yes."

'You see his awareness is increasing and he is relating better, so it was vital to me and him that he gain the extra year. I had a hard job convincing the Social Services on this issue.

'After my application was forwarded to them I had a visit from a lady representative on behalf of the Director of Social Services. This lady quietly informed me that he, the Director of Social Services, did not wish to extend Michael's stay and felt he would be better off placed in a local adult training centre. She went on to say that he felt Michael had been "away" from home long enough. I can listen to and accept advice, particularly if it is given from someone who has a knowledge of my boy, but this man had no in-depth knowledge of him, had spent no time with him. I wasn't going to have my son talked about like this as though he were a bloody number. Wait, it gets worse.' Rose lit a cigarette.

'When I put my arguments against this transfer she said that the Director suggested that I was frightened of Michael. That did it. I know, I exploded with anger and rage.

'Me, frightened of my own son. Nonsense, take that theory back where it came from. I just want him to have the best available help and what you are offering at present does not constitute that. Look, you go straight back to the Director himself and tell him to give me an appointment and I'll put my child's case to him myself. Just let me see him. The interview was over.'

As things turned out it was not necessary for Rose to see the Director. The headmistress had also sent in a strong plea in support of Michael's case and after months of what seemed to Rose arid reasoning and anxious waiting the DSS finally agreed to extend Michael's stay at boarding school. After regurgitating this section to me the recollection of it had visibly upset her somewhat. She organised her own recovery. 'We'll have those ham sandwiches now. I'll just have one cake, I don't want to lose my figure do I?'

Section 29 of the National Assistance Act of 1948 gave local authorities wide powers and a great deal of scope to provide help for the handicapped within their community through what was then known as the Welfare Services. This led to great variability of provision and help from region to region. Latterly, the Chronic Sick and Disabled Persons Act extended these powers and made it obligatory that authorities should 'seek out' and provide. This heralded a merging of departments which formerly included Welfare and Children's Departments as well as some aspects of Health Departments all under the huge umbrella that is now known as Social Services. On the whole most professional workers within the field welcomed the integration of these services, and what is large need not necessarily be ineffective or bad. Yet a service of any kind must seek to remain personalised no matter what its size. Clearly, what had upset Rose was the idea that she was no longer part of the dialogue which concerned her son's future. This was a maternal right that she could not suffer to place in abeyance and she reacted accordingly. In spite of the 'obligatory' clauses within the 'Chronically Sick and Disabled Act', provision and help vary enormously from local authority to local authority. At a time when 'cut back' is shrieked at Social Services Departments it might be as well for some of the lay surgeons of public spending to view precisely what they intend to lacerate.

'Michael is nineteen next month, last weekend he was telling me he would like a job at the zoo. He said he didn't mind what he did there as long as there were animals around. I suppose some of the animals couldn't be less hostile than some of the human beings he has come across. When I view his idea quite coldly there doesn't seem any realism to it but at least he is thinking outwardly. He does have a concept of the working world even though his choice is intensely selective. All I can do is maintain my hopes that this next year will see him improve even more. Of course, ideally, I would like him to enter the working world and be with us but I'm not over-optimistic about this.' Rose shook her head, slowly, sadly.

'Failing that, I'd hope to find some type of self-sufficient community which he can happily be part of and continue to learn the processes of living. Who knows, he could still continue to improve to the extent that he could manage present-day society. His independence is increasing slowly (he gets himself to Gravesend you know) and I think all the nurture he has received from all those who cared for him has made inroads into his withdrawn existence. I am sure he has not reached the ceiling of his potential yet.' These flashes of hope and statements of faith always cleared Rose's expression of the sadness of numerous retrospective problems or anxieties. She would then go further and pronounce what was tantamount to an affirmation. Not made to any special audience. Not made to me, but to herself.

'I will fight and fight to see that this progress is not thwarted – too much of my life has gone into it now, I could never give up. No, never. Can I type my little bit of this book?'

I looked at the knuckles of her hand. She had clenched the sides of the armchair whilst she was talking; she must have gripped the sides of the chair very tightly because the knuckles stood out sharp and white.

'Of course you can, Rose; you might have a problem deciphering my writing.'

'I'll manage, I have coped with worse things than that.'

There was no room for argument, and as I write this last sentence I feel chastened by her experiences. One's own petty anxieties become inane when parallelled with such adversity. How often does the suffering of someone else alleviate the by-stander or even the would-be helper? In this sense, offering help does not mean that any personal sacrifice is involved. Anyone helping Rose would probably receive more than they had given.

4
Margaret Estelle Gates

Margaret Estelle Gates, born Gravesend 1914, is the kind of 'dream material' that writers, with their capacity for predatory observation and interpretation, relish. Bits and pieces of her have flashed through novels, articles, travel books and books on education. At sixty-three, perhaps more than ever, she still commands one's attention. I have known her for fourteen years. I met her in a working situation. We were both teaching at a school for physically handicapped children in North London. It is difficult to make a self-evaluation, but at the time I was a competent, conscientious class teacher who was caring, but essentially also ambitious. For these qualities I was rewarded with what are termed as 'posts of special responsibility'; this meant an increase in salary as well as the prospects of eventual promotion. I needed to be liked by my colleagues and in consequence, I managed to achieve, through some diligence and some histrionics, a greater degree of skill in my work and a certain degree of charm. What I sorely lacked was any trace of humility.

This was probably why Margaret chose, for at least a year, to ignore me. She taught at the school for two days each week, specialising in needlework. Space was short in the building and for most of the time she worked in corridors or behind screens. She was a travelling lady in that she trundled her trolley and work materials into different spaces that the building could cough up. These difficult factors of her work did not seem to affect her; like a trained Bedouin she moved and journeyed about the building with an outwardly unperturbed grace, establishing order, routine and ritual wherever she was forced to settle.

Fortunately for me I managed to break out of the personal exile that she had chosen to place me in. School plays are often the subject for cartoonists' delight. However, I have to thank *Androcles and the Lion* for bringing Margaret and me together. The children required costumes and teachers were required to integrate their skills. Now she had to talk to me. I was the producer. We worked well together; this constituted a pleasant surprise for both of us and very slowly our friendship began from a mutual professional respect amidst the costumery. The friendship continued beyond the cotton threads that instigated it. Half-way through this period of hectic preparation, she was blissfully happy and exuberant. The forthcoming production was a minor contributing factor.

'I've got it. I can't believe it. I have never been lucky like this before. It was advertised in the *Evening Standard*. I went to see the lady. There were lots of people seeking the flat. Oh, what a marvellous woman, she was so nice to me.'

She held up her index finger and waved it slowly. This was one of her cautionary gestures which I have since seen many times over the years that have passed.

'She is no profiteer, this woman. The rent is so reasonable, and can you imagine it, a six-roomed flat in a mansion block. Six rooms, it's too much, I čan't believe it. I won't until I'm there.'

She did move to the huge flat in Chalk Farm and it wasn't until I saw where she had moved from that I completely appreciated her state of euphoria.

Her flat in Islington (if one could call it that) consisted of two rooms and a tiny kitchen. There was no bathroom and the lavatory was shared with several other tenants in the house. In these two rooms lived Margaret, her eldest daughter Diana, who was working, her nineteen-year-old son Peter, who was attending art college, and her youngest daughter Lisa, who was still at school. The rooms were small and perhaps these cramped conditions intensified Margaret's inherent sense of tidiness and preparation. Without these qualities no family could have survived the pressures of such an environment. Perhaps all of them haven't survived it. Margaret Gates up until this period had led what some may term 'a full life'. Others might view it all differently and others might consider it beyond interpretation. Her own childhood, she now reflects, was harsh but she talks of it with little trace of regret; there is a sad tone of acceptance to her anecdotes.

'I suppose that at the time you would consider us well-off compared with most families. We had a servant-cum-nanny and lived in a large house. My mother was very beautiful and most gentle. She had plenty to do in the house, but perhaps her greatest task was coping with my stepfather who was what was known as a naval recruiting officer. At work he was probably cool and efficient, but at home he was a handsome violent man who ruled the household with fearful tyranny. I can remember the abuse, both verbal and physical, that my mother received. Sometimes I could hear my mother crying as a result of his raging and maltreatment and I can remember lying in bed crying, staring at the winking night-lights, almost hypnotising myself into sleep. Once when my mother and I were leaving the house, he threw a broom at her from a top-floor window. I always wondered whether or not there was something symbolic about this action. Long after my parents were dead, an old aunt informed me of other significant factors which might have contributed towards the kind of household I was nurtured in.

'When I reached the age of sixty she informed me that the man who I had always believed was my stepfather was in fact my real father. Apparently, during her first marriage my mother had got a job as a barmaid. This caused great consternation and alarm amongst her relatives as it was considered to be an outrageous occupation for a person of my mother's background to take up. Her husband, a mild, sweet-tempered man, accepted this situation and suffered it quietly. My mother went even further on what was then considered to be a downward path by having a secret affair with one of her customers. Her husband did not know of this, or if he did, he chose to believe he did not know. My conception and birth came as a result of the extra-marital liaison. When I was five years old, my mother's husband died and she married the man who throughout his life was known to me as my stepfather. She could not have chosen a more different type of person. I suppose to some extent, I repeated the pattern myself in later years.'

She did. She married three times and had borne four children from the relationships. Separation and divorce ended the first two marriages and bereavement ended the last. All the men appear to make up a composite picture similar to the kind of men her mother had known. At the time that I met her all the children were reunited with her except for her eldest son, John. He was married and is still practising as a dental surgeon in Birmingham. It was this family entourage which moved into the flat in Hampstead. All of the children were blessed with their mother's skills in artistry and craft and together they transformed an old crumbling mansion flat into one of the most simple and beautiful homes that I have ever seen.

I first met Lisa (Margaret's youngest daughter) in an ice cream parlour when she was sixteen years of age. She was embarking on her 'O' level examinations and talked about the books she was reading, the teachers, the subjects she was worried about. She talked like most intelligent sixteen-year-old girls would talk. She seemed very tall, but this height added to her attractive open-featured face which was full of expression and animation. Her hair was blonde and long and her figure beautifully proportioned. There was a marvellous spontaneity to her conversation and a young fresh sense of humour which made our meeting bubble with laughter. We had quite a lot to talk about. I had been appointed as headteacher of a new school and her mother was joining my staff in a senior capacity. The future held promotion for both of us and Lisa was pleased. 'I'm not surprised Mum is going to work with you,' she said. I admit that at the time I was surprised. Ours had been a friendship born of circumstance and periodically we would choose to hurt one another with the kind of provocative conversation that lovers choose so that they can make amends afterwards. As we never chose to become lovers, reciprocal amendments were not always easy. I wondered how far Margaret would anticipate the difficulties that might arise in a new working situation. My fears were groundless and within the space of two years she had become my deputy headteacher. Her support in all areas was unbounding and she approached this last surprising pinnacle of her career with all the idealism and freshness of a young teacher.

This combination of skill and innocence are even sweeter now to me in retrospect. Our evenings after school were never or rarely spent together. It was the summer holidays which helped us discover as much about each other as we did of foreign peoples or territory. A six-week travelling holiday is an excellent acid test as to the permanence and meaning of any kind of relationship. We both chose to travel far and I could fill a book with anecdotes of our strange journeyings. Only one incident seems necessary to illustrate the strength of Margaret's principles.

On 8 August 1972 we were to be found in a small village on the edge of the Sahara. We had heard of the existence of the most extraordinary oasis some forty miles distant from the village. This oasis was described in the most evocative terms by the local populace. There were no tourists (apart from us) in the village and the route to this place of enchantment was merely an ill-defined track across miles of sand. We stared at the sand in the early hours of the morning and concluded that we would go without any discussion, just a nod of the head. Early risers never feel the need to talk much. However, before leaving there was a debate. 'They are not worth it.' I looked at the four small oranges that the old Arab vendor held before us. 'You're wrong.' It was clear that Margaret was intent on purchase. We always shared expenses to the last detail. For some mean, irrational reason I stubbornly rejected the orange contract. 'Well I'm not bothering with them,' I said, leaving her to decide whether or not she would buy. It was a challenge which she took up. 'You are quite sure you don't want them?' I nodded. She spoke as the oranges were being handed over to her. 'I'm not going to share these with you.' I shrugged off her response with smiling indifference and made my way towards the dusty Renault. Margaret took the wheel, the fruit was cast under her seat, and within minutes the fractious finance arrangements of the morning were forgotten as we bumped our way through a landscape of sand and sky. Progress was unbelievably slow and by mid-day our mileage was considerably less than anticipated – by any calculation we were less than half way from our destination. At this stage not surprisingly I felt hot and parched. Margaret felt much the same and relieved her discomfort by sucking an orange.

There was no point in asking for the smallest portion, the principles had to be adhered to, we both knew this. My discomfort was further increased by a dust storm which seemed to come from nowhere and stopped our progress completely. Just when I was beginning to fantasise on the prospects of dying from thirst it went away. To our enormous relief we reached the oasis just before dark. There were three households inhabiting it and all offered us shelter. The darkness came almost immediately as the inevitable mint tea was placed before us. I scalded my tongue in my anxiety to relieve what had now become an aching thirst. In the meantime, Margaret sipped her tea tranquilly, safe in the knowledge that a spare orange remained under the driving seat in the car.

Visiting her in her present state of retirement, I am left with chequered memories of this nature and it is difficult to imagine that any kind of holocaust either human or of the elements could daunt the strength of such a woman. One day in school she came to my room, placed her glasses on my desk, rubbed her eyes and looked at me in a blank way that I had not seen before.

'Lisa has been diagnosed as schizophrenic,' she said.

At the time, my instant concern was for the lovely young girl that I had met in the ice cream shop. I had no way of knowing how such an illness could debilitate and slash away the energies and drive of a mother like Margaret. Its effect on her over a period of two years was devastating to behold, yet she still maintains a gravity and balance in the face of the most appalling odds stacked against her.

A handicap which is either acquired late, or manifests itself much later than the first few years of childhood must present a mother with as many problems as it does the afflicted person. In Margaret's case, the issue has clearly affected what remains of the rest of her life. By the time Lisa was seventeen, Margaret's other children could be termed as reasonably happy and settled – the eldest, John, still practising dentistry in Birmingham within the framework of his own family; Diana enjoying her work as a landscape gardener; Peter now a successful designer, married, housed comfortably and the proud father of a young baby daughter. But left with Margaret is Lisa. 'It's no good looking for a straight interview from me, you know most of it all anyway.' She stopped. 'No you don't, nobody does. You will just have to keep coming around, I'll meander when I talk and if you can you will just have to knock the bits into some sort of shape. I'm not enjoying retirement, I thought I might, I'm occupied.'

'You can say that again.'

She was sitting on a low divan in her large bed-sitting-room. She was surrounded by handbags, some completed, some with pins in them waiting for different kinds of wooden handles. Each bag was individually designed and entirely hand-made. Margaret pointed to them.

'See what I'm doing?' She talked as she sewed. 'I suppose Lisa's illness started when she was about seventeen and a half. I can't quite put my finger on it, but there was a way she had of answering questions. Somehow, the answers weren't strictly on line. They weren't ambiguous answers, just puzzling. Yes, very puzzling. Then there were the odd bursts of hysteria which seemed to have no valid basis. One hoped it was some kind of adolescent phase. The outbursts increased and you. . . .'

Margaret stopped talking, put the half-completed bag on the divan and took a sheaf of notes from the shelf above her. 'I took these notes this morning.' She passed them to me.

'On entering the kitchen at six a.m. this morning.

'Lisa's conversation: "A Mars Bar a day keeps the – away –. Put that in your pipe Dad and smoke it. I broke my maidenhead on a horse – they shoot horses don't they – up yours – you bastard. I'm a lesbian – I'm in the pudding club – I'm a tea-leaf, do you know what that is? I'm reaching for the best, I'm reaching. But I want to teach. Can I be a teacher Mum? Fucking Eddie – David the bastard – Richard the Lion Heart – not half. I'm a bitch – oh, dear, no hanky panky. I know, no I don't know – I'm on the way out you know – I'm in my prime. I'm staying in – put that in your pipe and smoke it Tut-ankh-amen – so you see the world is round – it's got bells on – you're a dark horse. I get the picture and the exorcist – I'm corrupted. I'm going to heaven when I die, I'm the eternal Peter Pan. Do I look nice Mum? Do me a lemon Mum, I can't stop going to the toilet. Eddie is nice, he's a bastard, I shall hit him ever so hard. I don't need to be forgiven Mum – you do – I forgave you Mum even before I was born. Oh, well Tut-ankh-amen isn't dead. I'm going to buy some peanut butter and some milk, or four pints, a pint a day will keep the blokes away. Nudge, nudge, wink, wink. I do. I do." (Laughs loudly.) "Ah, John's a dark horse – I really love him – heaven help us all. I'm going to get a job and I'm not going to prison – the law can't touch me – I love him Jim Davis and Jim Davis and Jim Davis. Oh God. Leave me alone. Christoff – he's driving me mad. Mum can I have that bag?" (Pointing to my bag) "You've got the most beautiful hands I have ever, ever seen in my life. If you don't leave me alone Christoff – give me a lemon Christoff. They're all the same. I'm a seeker. They are sexually deprived like you and Peter Brooke. He haunts me you know." (She takes my last bit of tobacco.) "You shouldn't be mean you know. Rita is a casualty – yeah so what! I've turned over a new leaf Mum." (Giggles.) "I'm not a bitch Christoff; you are. You'd better be careful Mum my friends are going to rob this place. Will you leave this radio to me in your will? Thank you. Jamie, he's my best friend. I'm my best friend – I'm not my worst enemy. He ain't heavy – he's my brother – I want my brother Pete's baby – desperately. You're great Mum – you're fantastic – you're going to die soon, Dad's the eternal Peter Pan – I wish you'd do something about him, I will but I can't yet. Oh, Mum, I'm afraid – I'm going to ignore you Mum. I've had a red-head before I'm dead – I'm having a red-headed baby. Yeah, Mum I'm sorry. If the price of bacon goes up, pigs will fly. I feel sick – I'm going to be ill – oh, leave me alone – I can't do what ten people tell me."

'(Me): "Who's the ten people?"

"Everybody – I'm going to have ten kids Mum, if not fifteen. Are you defrosting the fridge Mum? I'll do it for you." (Puts the record player on very loud 7.00 a.m. and will not turn it down. She allows me to do it, hugs me and sobs.) "Mum, I love you I feel like Laurel and Hardy." (I hear her sobbing in the next room. I make some cocoa and coax her to have a sleep. She agrees, but a few minutes later comes in, she is wearing different clothes ready to go out.) "Bacon's not good for you – you ought to know that because you're Jewish. Nice to know you Mum." (Goes out.)

'You see it is difficult to plan a strategy of help, one goes from one day to the next or one hopes for a calmer period. They do come sometimes. Look, here is one of her notes.'

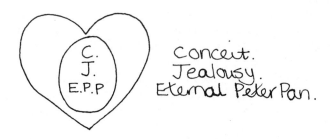

The oval in the heart represents the world and the curse is on me to find out what's wrong in the world. But I'm so unaware. (That's what I seem to be), I'm not really because the curse makes me aware. The curse isn't known about until I'm dead. And because I'm aware and people don't think I am, I wonder and pause and meditate on why they talk to me the way they do. I've just worked this out. I never realised it before. I'm unaware of what people mean (in what way it was meant) when they say something to me. Because of that I can't accept being loved or give love either, or just love. A force field electricity all around me stops people's vibrations from reaching me. But I don't know why it is there. Other people's vibrations never reach me (Tut-ankh-amen's my guide). The message never really registers in my brain. My body lost in legend and because of that, every man who wants to make love to me never gets me going. People all over the world must listen when I show them what is wrong.

'How old is Lisa now Margaret?' I asked.
'She is twenty-five. You remember her as a young girl?'
At this point, Lisa came in and offered to make me a cup of tea. I wasn't sure that the tea would arrive, but it did and Lisa talked with me – calm, lucid and seemingly happy. From this meeting it was difficult to relate this young woman to her mother's early-morning account or the note that she had left for her mother. However, I remembered a week's holiday spent in Majorca three or four years previously which gave me a sharp reminder of the hazard and strain that Lisa could evoke.

A friend of Diana (Margaret's eldest daughter) had kindly offered us the use of a villa in a tiny village some fourteen miles distant from Palma. We visited Palma once. This was enough for all of us. It was crowded with Whitsuntide visitors. At this time Lisa was about twenty years of age and her schizophrenia had begun to declare itself in a much more pronounced fashion than Margaret had indicated earlier. Margaret felt the four of us (who enjoyed good rapport) would, with the peaceful surroundings of the villa, alleviate in some way the problems with which both she and Lisa were confronted. In short, she went to Majorca with Lisa because she hoped it might 'do Lisa good'.

My reasons for accompanying them were not motivated by compassion. My first novel was incubus in my head and I erroneously concluded that I would be able to translate the thoughts and ideas to words more easily outside the usual environs of my kitchen. We settled into the villa quickly. It was a large spacious house with bedrooms to spare after we had all been accommodated separately. We soon moulded into a very gentle domestic routine, household chores such as cleaning and cooking being shared without any acrimony as there was so little to do. Lisa was given an open option to help if she wanted to – she did sometimes share these chores with whoever was undertaking them. However, I remember her joining me on several occasions only to drift off without a word leaving the half-peeled carrot and the knife behind her, almost as though what she had been doing was part of a dream or not part of her.

Other days gave me what can only be termed as practical or visual illuminations as to the extent of her illness. Diana had suggested that, as an act of good will towards the landowner of the villa, we might rid its forecourt of the rampant weeds which were approaching it in the most prolific and relentless manner. I do not like gardening, much less weeding, and I feigned a headache and lay in the shade of the verandah of the house whilst Diana and Margaret were working. I watched them work and felt irksome and angry. I had come here to write, not to weed a bloody garden. Of course, I put out of my head the fact that up to this moment I could only write in the early morning or between nine and eleven in the evening. I lay there suffering. Some might say that my behaviour was irrational, others might term it neurotic. I was feeling apathetic, indecisive and unhappy, but I was aware of my surroundings.

At some stage of my self-inflicted anxiety I turned on my side and was surprised to see Lisa lying flat on the cold tiled floor. She was lying so still, eyes staring up at the ceiling, that my first thoughts were that she was having a fit.

'Lisa, Lisa,' I called out to her. At first she did not answer. I got up from the divan and walked to her side. I spoke quietly this time.

'Lisa, Lisa.' I hesitated a little and wondered whether or not to fetch Margaret in from the forecourt. Then Lisa slowly placed her arm across her forehead and I felt relieved. She spoke, but not to me.

'I'm a banjo Tut-ankh-amen. I'm a banjo. I'm bango.'

She then broke into peals of laughter and rolled over on the floor before lying quite still once again. It was then that I realised that Lisa was unaware of all of us. There was some private world which we could not comprehend or even enter. I left her and joined Margaret and Diana in the garden tugging fiercely at the thistles. Diana said I ought to put some gloves on, but in all truth at that moment I was glad that I could feel the prickles. Margaret must have sensed some motivation for my action, some disruption or assault on my previous inertia.

'Has Lisa said anything to you?'

'No,' I replied truthfully. 'She has said nothing to me.'

In some ways being accountable or responsible for Lisa throughout this week was rather like dealing with a five-year-old child as far as decisions were concerned. On one hand we did not feel that we should be too restrictive, but on the other hand there were areas where we all felt the need to be protective. Lisa would make gestures to the effect that she would like to accept some part of the domestic responsibility of the running of the household. We had exhausted our supply of potatoes. Lisa offered to go and buy some, she was not asked. We gave her some pesetas and I think all of us felt some misgivings as she left the house shortly before mid-day to make her purchase. There was only one shop which was not more than 600 yards distant from us.

I expressed agitation and concern first. This was not because I cared more, but because I had known less experience of such similar situations. Margaret and Diana had gone through all this kind of tense waiting before.

After two hours Lisa had still not appeared.

'We must do something,' I wailed.

Margaret suggested we should wait a further fifteen minutes and then act. She lit and smoked a cigarette and made tea for all of us. In the midst of clearing away the crockery she announced her strategy.

'One of us must stay here at base, one of us must comb the village – ask in every house, shop, café or workplace if they have seen her. One of us must walk each lane that leads from the village up to three or four miles and keep asking everyone they meet if they have seen her. I am not contacting the police, only as a last resort, it is difficult enough explaining Lisa's illness in Britain let alone here in Spain.'

Diana set out to explore the lanes. I investigated the village and Margaret took on the worst option of looking after the base. As far as I was concerned any activity was easier than the fearful waiting.

I called at every house, every smallholding – I had this bucolic idea that I would see Lisa feeding rabbits with cabbage leaves and pursued my quest for her in the hope of looking forward to my sense of relief. It never came. Garage owners shook their heads, the people in the café conversed and then frowned negatively, even the blacksmith at the forge was questioned. The church held two old women in black who seemed cross with me for entering it so noisily. I returned to the villa three hours later hoping to find her there. I was greeted by Margaret. She was alone. Diana got back looking drawn, tired and exhausted two hours later. Neither of us talked much, but Margaret, unlike me, did not despair.

'It's nearly dark. Put on all the lights, Diana, all of them so that she can see the place. I'll telephone the police and we will have to report her missing. I don't think anything too horrible could happen on an island of this size.' She sighed and picked up the telephone. She seemed to be having a great deal of difficulty in getting through to the operator. When she did get through, she could not hear or be heard. A huge lorry had stopped outside the house, its engine was left chugging at a great rate and this reverberated through the house to such an extent that the windows rattled. We heard voices, men's voices and then there was a peal of laughter.

'That's Lisa,' said Diana.

Margaret replaced the telephone receiver and we all went to the front of the house. Lisa stood at the gate and was waving to the lorry which was pulling slowly away. She turned towards us and smiled a greeting. At her feet was a hundred-weight sack of potatoes.

For the rest of the holiday Lisa gave us slender cause for trepidation. There were moments of discomfort like the time she chose to give one of the oldest men I have ever seen a spontaneous and long kiss. I thought he was going to faint with alarm or rage and he mumbled at us in Spanish. We got Lisa back to our table in the café.

'What did you do that for? The poor bloke didn't understand did he?'

'I felt sorry for him. You don't have to understand that,' she said.

We all left Majorca looking and feeling refreshed; even at this point I was marvelling at Margaret's resilience and was convinced that no illness however fierce could break it. Thanks to Lisa we had all also managed to put on weight.

Margaret pursued every course open to her in order to find some way of helping Lisa. However, the strain of the undertaking began to show on her and for the first time in my life I saw her beginning to look not only physically but emotionally fatigued. Inevitably, one sunny day she told me that Lisa had been admitted to hospital. From the outset Margaret could only view the measure as temporary.

'Dr Mayer my GP has given me enormous support. I'm not religious as you know, but if there is a saint on earth, then he is the one. He has helped me at every turn, but her illness seems to be deepening. I have tried to cope with all the shocks and turmoil as they have come, but this thing has left me in terror for my own daughter's life.' (Lisa had made a suicide attempt and had slashed her wrists.) 'I have never felt comfortable about the idea of hospitalisation, but this time there really was no choice. Lisa has been admitted to Friern Barnet Hospital. I am going to see her as often as I can.'

Margaret visited almost every day after working a full day at school. I accompanied her on several occasions and on each and every one could only marvel at the strength of purpose behind each visit.

'If I don't visit I am afraid she may retreat further and further away. I listen for most of the time and sometimes there are flashes of the daughter that I once knew.'

Lisa remained at Friern Barnet for seven months. It is difficult to ascertain whether or not this stay brought about any improvement in her condition. The times that I visited her she mixed praise with complaint. She enjoyed the pottery classes and there were some 'great' people in Friern. She did not like the more institutionalised activities such as packing Christmas cards and dismantling telephones.

'The people that have been here for years and years don't seem to mind it, but me, I get itchy feet and get bored. Then the voices tell me I should leave here.'

Lisa expressed her disenchantment by disappearing for a day or two; she would turn up at home and then eventually go back to the hospital. Given the enormous demands that were made on the staff by all the patients, Lisa could not have been the easiest of people to help. One factor was clear during this period and that was that at least Margaret's health had begun to improve. An evening of uninterrupted sleep was a luxury to her and for a time the intensity of stress which she had formerly carried was held in abeyance.

Her 'rest period' was ended almost as traumatically as the incident which had instigated its commencement.

'One afternoon after I had visited Lisa I was called into the office. I thought that perhaps they were going to discuss some new course of treatment. "Lisa is discharged," they said. Just like that. There was nothing more I could do but take her home with me. I suppose I could have just given up there and then, just throw my hands in the air and say I could take no more. I do feel like that still, but it is not in my nature to give up and I had to find Lisa some sort of alternative to the provisions at Friern. In all honesty, I don't think that I have the resources to help her much at home. She was with me for two and a half months before I could find anywhere else.'

It is a common fallacy that aid and help is plonked on a plate for mothers in similar situations to Margaret. There are telephone numbers given, addresses bandied around, suggestions made, but more often than not the particular mother concerned must pursue her aims with the ruthless singularity of a detective. I can remember Margaret throughout this period, the visits, the correspondence, the telephone calls. 'Hello, yes, this is Mrs Gates, yes, M. E. Gates. I wonder if you could help me. . . .'

In the past, before Lisa's illness had blighted Margaret's effervescence and contagious sense of wonder, she would often hold many of the staff spellbound with her anecdotes about travel, something she had seen, or some person she had met. She had an extraordinary facility for passing on experiences. She talked less nowadays and felt that she did not want to be 'boring people' with her endless domestic tales of woe. It was good to hear the hopefulness in her voice once again. We all listened to her and all hoped (or prayed) that the future was going to be brighter. 'I've done it, oh, my God, I can't believe it. Places are like gold dust in this type of hostel. But they are giving a place to my Lisa. It's in Reading – less than an hour's journey from London. I know that there have been some terrific achievements in these places. It's not a hospital, but a place which is part of the community.' I watched her as she talked. The animation in the telling of her plans seemed to disperse the worried, drawn, perplexed look that we had come to accept as her permanent expression.

Lisa had been offered a place in a hostel run by the Richmond Fellowship and Margaret had gratefully accepted it and Lisa had agreed to attend. Margaret's relief was short-lived. The hostel had only newly been opened and was probably going through its first teething troubles. Lisa co-operated badly and frequently ran home. Margaret felt there was some division of opinion between the two people running the hostel as to how they could best achieve their aims. Inevitably Lisa was once again discharged. Margaret accepted it more philosophically the second time around. She shrugged her shoulders and said, 'I can't blame them really, how can they treat or help someone if she's not there? So there it is, seven months at Friern Barnet and four months with the Richmond Fellowship and now I am back to where I started from.'

From my observation at the time, Margaret's last statement was not entirely true. She was not back to where she started from, but further back. The fifteen months that followed this period were probably the bleakest. In terms of stress, it was most harsh and this took its toll on Margaret's health. I had worked with Margaret Gates for many years and over this period of time I had come to the conclusion that she was the healthiest person I had ever known. At sixty she was still in charge of girls' games and could get round the netball pitch with the agility of an adolescent girl. She took swimming and never sat at the side of the baths. She would feel hurt if she did not take part in the school journey – a strenuous around-the-clock activity by any standards. She was never late and never absent. Odd day or occasional absences were unknown to her attendance record. However, after Lisa's discharge from the Richmond Fellowship Hostel we watched Margaret disintegrate both physically and emotionally. Fortunately ours is a workplace where adults can cry and not feel ashamed. What was so dreadful for all of us was that we were impotent as far as offering constructive help was concerned. It came as no surprise to us when she was absent from school. Nervous exhaustion was the phrase used for the illness; by any standards it is a descriptive understatement of what we witnessed.

'I have had good times throughout my life and bad times, but nothing could compare to this. It was fearful, terrible – I can't describe the horror of it all. I couldn't keep Lisa locked in the flat all day, nor could I accompany her everywhere that she chose to go. By any standards she is vulnerable and most people could quickly recognise this. Somehow she got to know a group of druggies who were living in a "squat" near the Roundhouse. Then one thing happened after another and I just couldn't keep up with facing crisis after crisis. On top of this, or at the same time it was all happening, the stealing began. She must have robbed almost every flat in the block, not valuable things, but silly absurd articles which were of no use to her whatsoever. This did not assuage the anger of some of the victims, but many of them were most understanding when I explained the situation. Kleptomania was something I had not had to deal with before and I felt as though I was in perpetual hazard.'

She was in hazard. Her flat was ransacked and there were threats and bangings on the door from all kinds of people through the night into the early hours of the morning. It reached fever pitch at one stage and Margaret telephoned me in abject terror for her life.

'Tom, I can't cope any more, I'm sorry, but would you mind staying here for a few days. I'm frightened. I would feel better if there were someone else here.'

It was a relief to be able to do something which would alleviate the strain for her, and I suggested a 'rota scheme' for a short period. I would stay with her some nights and a mutual friend and colleague, Geoff Howitt, would stay when I was not there. When I explained the matter, his response was immediate. It was positive with no prevarication. In the past he and I had had what could be termed as 'differences'. These were dispersed when we were confronted with a 'gut' situation. In contrast, all our disagreements seemed unnecessary and silly and this situation brought about a lasting reconciliation. Helping someone else often does this, it's a bit like darning a sock, only one realises that there should never have been a hole there in the first place. I contacted Margaret and relayed the good news.

'We will alternate this week, I hope the heavy ones come when Geoff is there. He is bigger than I am.'

After a week we discussed it all.

'This business will kill Maggie,' Geoff said, gulping a light ale. I wanted to disagree with him, but from what I had gleaned I felt that to all intents and purposes his assumption was correct. It nearly killed her, but not quite.

'I suppose all the terror and desperation that I felt reached the point of no return with a spate of suicide attempts interspersed with violence. Lisa became very aggressive and attacked us with knives and I felt that I could not contain or restrain her in any sense. I went to the Maudsley Hospital and begged. Yes, begged them to take her in. At first they wouldn't consider it after I had stayed there all night pleading. Eventually, they agreed on the basis that it would remove her from the dangers of the "drug scene" which she had encountered.' Margaret smiled cynically.

'It was a short respite. She had not been there for more than three weeks before they sent her home. My GP received a letter to say that Lisa was not really ill at all, but "merely difficult". Oh, my God, merely difficult! This diagnosis was like a spear going through me. I wrote letters to all kinds of people – including my MP – but nothing came from all my pleas. It was left to Dr Mayer to help me again. The demands I have made on that dear man just cannot be recorded. Do you know he has never expressed exasperation, never indicated that I was a nuisance, never flinched in his support. He is golden. For the first time Lisa was admitted to hospital against her will. She was admitted to the Royal Free a month after leaving the Maudsley. I felt dreadful about this gesture, but there were no other options open to me. In fact, if I had not agreed to this admission, I think that I would have ended up in hospital myself. This was pointed out to me by my closest friends.

'Dr Mayer arranged the admission and I helped Lisa pack her belongings with a heavy heart. Hope was something I no longer possessed.'

It was in this state of mind that Margaret returned to her work at school. After one week it was patently obvious that this was not the woman we had once known. All the teaching skills were there, but the zest had been torn from her. She had realised this herself and quietly informed me that she felt that she would be obliged to retire. Apart from the economic sacrifice involved there was an emotional one too.

'I have grown to love this place, the people, the kids, all of it and I am happy in this job and there aren't many people who can say that. But I know I can't manage this and Lisa. She comes first now, the present situation is only temporary and I must plan for her future not mine. I don't know how it will all end, but it seems to me now that I have another full-time job on my hands coping with her needs.'

I said that she should think it all over. She did this, and three weeks later handed in her resignation.

I received it and it was formally forwarded through all the usual administrative channels. Yet somehow I never quite came to terms with the idea that she was leaving. In a practical sense I had conceded, but emotionally I was not reconciled to the reality. It was not until the final homage was being effected that I accepted the fact that she would be gone from us. An informal gathering was arranged. Concluding speeches were to be made by me, the Chairman of the Governors, and Margaret. Lectures and public speaking I enjoy, but like many others, I prefer to prepare what I am going to say. Our Chairman made a sensitive appraisal of Margaret's work but when it came to my turn, I found it most difficult. I had not prepared it because I had not believed it could happen. I don't know whether I cried on my behalf or hers, but after the public weeping I could talk more easily. Margaret, as one would expect, had prepared her l'envoy.

Shortly before this farewell gathering, Lisa had been discharged from the Royal Free Hospital. This time she arrived home with less trauma and the discharge was not hurled in Margaret's face. Some preparation was involved before her daughter finally left the hospital.

'I had no complaints, she really did come home in a very much more settled state. Lisa had been stabilised by the use of certain drugs and she was a lot better than when she had entered the hospital. There was no doubting that. You might think I am hard, but I did not want her back home.' Margaret shook her head and frowned. 'I had very good reasons.'

She used her index finger on the fingers of her other hand to list the reasons. They all seemed valid to me.

(a) 'Stabilising her on drugs is only half of the cure – or does it just keep the illness at bay and effect no real cure? It does offer more immediate help, but what does it hold out for the future? Babies would never grow teeth unless they are weaned from their mothers' breasts; they need other interests or else mother would be a walking milk bar all her life.'

(b) 'Lisa at this stage needed some urgent form of motivation to give her a more definite rapport with life and people. She really needed a hostel with the right kind of provision that could give her a reason for living.'

(c) 'I don't want to criticise any aspects of occupational therapy such as basket-making, etc., it is all useful in its way, but in Lisa's case, although her mind is disorientated or disturbed, it's alert and I do understand that she would quickly become bored by repetitive activities.'

(d) 'On leaving the Royal Free she was ready for the next step, step forward, helping hand. Call it what the hell you like, but, she wanted and needed to be trained or taught for something useful.

'The people at the hospital did not disagree with me that Lisa was in need of such a hostel placement, they just informed me that all such hostels were full and over-subscribed with a waiting list. To be fair to the hospital they did try, but always the same answers come back: "Sorry, full up, long waiting list." One's first reaction is to be angry with the people who forward this kind of negative information, but really it is not their fault and I feel sorry for them in some ways because they bear the brunt, venom and spleen of those who are genuinely seeking help or provision from sources which either do not exist or are pathetically inadequate. Sometimes, after being angry in these kind of situations, I have often said, "Look I'm sorry, I know it's not your fault, but you can understand how I feel can't you?" Usually they understand.'

By this time Margaret had reached a point whereby her judgment as to what was the correct place for Lisa was impaired by her own physical ʰealth and state of mind. It is not surprising that she found that she could only sleep for short, fitful intervals before waking with some fresh anxiety on her mind. For the first time in her life sleeping tablets became a necessity. Until this period of prolonged crisis such a prescription would have been completely alien to her outlook and attitudes. In the present situation it became imperative that she got some hours of sleep and rest one way or another.

'I can only think that desperation led me to agree to her being sent to a home in Ipswich which I had come to know about. I suppose even geriatric homes differ in the kind of provision they offer. Like schools, hospitals or any other establishment may vary. Some geriatric homes are bound to offer the right kind of stimuli that the folks in them require. I was horrified when I first saw the place that was to be my Lisa's home; it wasn't a geriatric centre but it felt like one. Everyone there seemed to sit in chairs from the time they got up almost until it was time to go to bed again. Poor Lisa, I think she genuinely tried to make a go of things and make the best of it all, but I do understand her attempts to resist the placement there. She must have felt as though she had reached the end of the road. I would get telephone calls from all kinds of places, towns that I had not heard of, or large railway stations where she had been found wandering, bereft, ill-clad and oh, so very vulnerable. So, inevitably she arrived home again. She celebrated her first evening by overdosing herself to the point where we had to get her back to the hospital once again. She recovered and, as you know, she has been here ever since.'

October 1976, I look at Margaret in 'retirement', surrounded by the hand-sewn handbags which take up what she has left of spare time. I listen and still the optimism squeezes through in between the sighs and expressions of anguish and anger.

'Lisa's gone through a good patch these last two months, as long as I get her to Dr Mayer for her Modecate, she seems to be at least a bit more level. I don't think that is the only reason though. You know, the young bloke called Rufus? Well, he has really tried to help her. OK he has problems of his own and people with problems are drawn to other people with problems and on it all goes. But in his case, I have watched him improve – silly word to use. I agreed that he could stay here on some evenings with Lisa. I know some people would throw up their hands in horror to hear of such a thing. Oh, dear God, I think there is more hypocrisy uttered about sex than anything else. Anyway, I cannot complain about his relationship with Lisa. Do you know he has got himself a job? He sweeps the street. There is nothing shameful in that, and what is more he is not disliking it. He even tried to persuade Lisa into doing something like it.' Margaret paused.

'I would be deliriously happy if she could achieve that, not for economic reasons, but just for the idea that she would be nearer some activity which was real and tangible. She refused and I'm afraid that she is treating him rather badly at the moment. I hope the relationship doesn't founder on the rocks because it is proving just as stabilising as any drug. But you can't feed someone a relationship can you?'

As she talked, she noticed my puzzled expression as I scanned several miles of cardboard boxes stacked against the sides of the wall opposite me. They were neatly tied and labelled – 'crockery', 'my books', 'Diana's books', 'tinned food'.

'We are moving,' she said.

'Where on earth to? You're not leaving London are you?'

She laughed. 'Hardly, my dear, it's the shortest move in history. Ten yards to be precise; we have to move to the flat across the hall. It is only temporary. I wonder how long "temporary" will be?' she mused.

'You remember I mentioned the original owner of this place?' I nodded. 'Nice lady, well she had to sell this block of flats. I am sure she was forced to because of financial difficulties. They were then bought up by a company who really tried to get some of us out by gentle persuasion. I don't think any families were stupid enough to leave, although some of them might have done. It was a relief to hear that the council had purchased us all because this place was becoming terribly run-down. The lift hasn't worked for years, but I don't mind the stairs, it's all good for the lungs. It is a bit of a heave if you are carrying shopping though.'

She gestured towards the boxes with her hand. 'Well, they are modernising us now, it will mean central heating and a rise in rent. I don't like either very much – I mean the central heating or the rent rise. I am quite happy with my paraffin heaters, but what can you do? I know that the heating bills will soar and all the time I have to think in terms of money, money, money.'

The cost of keeping a person like Lisa far outweighs the allowances that are given. At present Lisa receives £7.60 invalidity pension and £1.80 from supplementary benefit. The grand total amounts to £9.40. Earlier on I described Lisa at sixteen. The tall, slim girl bears no resemblance to the young woman that I view today. Lisa has put on a great deal of weight. In part this must be due to her eating habits, which are more regular than most people's and certainly more frequent. The 'snacks' seem to be part of her day as well as ordinary meal times. She will also get up in the early hours of the morning and munch her way through any food that she might find available. I believe the over-eating is just one other manifestation of her illness – it is an expensive one. Possessions seem to have little meaning for Lisa. Margaret has mentioned her kleptomania, but Lisa gives more away than she takes. A coat, a cardigan or even shoes are quite suddenly not around any more: 'I think I gave them to someone, Mum, they really needed them.' Margaret is the only one available to reimburse the loss. There is no choice for her.

'When I take Lisa to the doctor, I can use my free travel pass (I'm an old-age pensioner, darling), but Lisa's fare is fifty pence return. There can be no question of her missing the visit because without her drugs I couldn't manage her here at all.'

Apart from her allowance, Lisa must cost Margaret at least £15 each week – this she must supplement from her retirement pension. There can be precious little left of it. 'One thing about having a daughter like Lisa around is that you have to look ahead. I don't suppose that I would ever have become the kind of old lady who busied herself attending classes in flower arrangement. In a way I have to be almost like a seventeen-year-old – each day comes and I make of it what I can, the future on so many levels is so uncertain. Only death is certain and I have to think about that. Not in any moribund way, but in terms of what happens to Lisa when I am not here. Look, I'm no collapsed ruin, I'm fit now, but for how much longer will I be operative? I know Diana will do what she can for Lisa after I am gone, but all of that is not as simple as it sounds. My eventual death does not hold fears for me, yet unless I can organise certain details before it happens I will carry fears for my daughter's life with me to the grave.

'I'll name just one item, I could go through ten of them. What happens to this flat when I die? Does the tenancy pass to my eldest daughter Diana? If not, where can she find accommodation on her own in London – let alone accept some accountability and responsibility for Lisa? If they allow the tenancy to transfer to Diana, it will still be tough going for her; if they don't then God help my daughters because I cannot see how they can manage.' She shook her head and added with a tone of quiet conviction, 'No I can't.

'I don't want to talk about it all any more. Do you mind?'

I shook my head.

'Oh, make it clear will you that I don't have any complaints about any of the people or places where Lisa has been. They are all working under pressure, almost in a state of siege if you like. We know what it is like working under pressure don't we? I can't come to terms with how angry I feel about provision for people like Lisa. The shortage of staff, the shortage of places – and what do shallow phrases like "community care" mean if it is not existent? Because there isn't a place for her, Lisa is doomed to spend each day, every day in the flat. I am here some of the time, but whether I am here or not, she is ostensibly alone. She is without real friends and without any incentive to go anywhere with a real objective in mind. When she does leave the flat it is usually only to wander. Her concentration isn't sustained for any length of time, so reading, sewing or even listening to records are sporadic activities. Now we hear that it is cut-back time and that we must all tighten our belts. Can it mean a further cut in provision? Surely not. Governments and local authorities must realise the importance of proper care and supervision for people like Lisa. Even in economic terms patch-work help is a poor investment because like a house without foundations, it leaves the core of the problem still there. If left long enough then the place falls down. I suppose only first-hand experience could illuminate the problem. We have had deaf MPs and blind ones – if one developed schizophrenia do you think matters might improve?'

She offered me a glass of Dubonnet (her one luxury) and cautioned me not to drink it all at once and said that I should make it last.

'Here, did you know that I am coming out of retirement next week? Barbara is ill in hospital and won't be able to go on the school journey to the Lake District. I am going up there – Diana has said she will look after Lisa.'

'It is a bit wet and cold at this time of the year, Margaret.'

'Oh, I don't mind the rain and it will be a pleasure for me. I do miss the kids you know.'

I returned home to see the following report in the *Guardian*. It has unnerved me and made me feel that I could write nothing more about Margaret Estelle Gates.

The *Guardian*, 15 October 1976

£¼M SCHOOL EMPTY
By Dennis Johnson

A school for 130 educationally subnormal children, just completed in Tewkesbury, at a cost of £250,000, will stand empty for at least a year because Gloucestershire County Council does not have enough money to run it.

Parents in north Gloucestershire have complained for years that there is not enough provision for backward children in their area.

But now the council finds that, because of spending cuts, it cannot afford the £50,000 needed to run the new school in the present financial year.

The county education department had hoped that, for the time being, it could provide extra accommodation for the eight-form entry Tewkesbury Comprehensive School, on the same site. But the head, Mr. J. C. Faull, and the governors, claim it would be unsuitable.

Beginning

One in six children born in this country will have a handicap of one kind or another. The severity of the handicap will vary and the stress it engenders on the particular parents will be individual to them. With most, or almost all, mothers there is an initial shock on discovery and then perhaps a resistance to there being anything wrong, and then finally an acceptance of the situation. This acceptance is not a curtain which is drawn across the future performances of their children. It is in fact the beginnings of deeper awareness of their child's needs and for many of the parents it is tantamount to the beginnings of a lifetime of questioning and research on behalf of their offspring. It is clear that when a handicap is apparent or begins to manifest itself, then it is easier for the parent concerned if they are told sensitively and frankly about the implication of the present and given some prognosis as to what the future may hold. However, as we can see from some of the accounts that have gone before, this is not as simple as it may sound.

Few mothers in this situation look for a magic wand which if waved will put all things right. On the other hand, they do look for chinks of light which can lead them and their children a little further forward. Many of them are forced to be great architects and builders and no one can argue that some of the bridges that they have built across rivers of debility would confound professional opinion. Unlike professional workers in this field, they are not paid to care. How such a mother cares will cause some problems for the person who is paid to help them. So much has been written about guilt feelings of parents that one can spend the whole time ascribing all their feelings and reactions to these 'feelings' and that is that. Unless they are making the mother ill, why not say, 'OK you have guilt feelings, so what? So have I? Now we know this, let's have a look at your next suggestion.' From my experience it would seem the 'guilt' issue is heavily over-subscribed, many parents react in what would seem to be an irrational manner not from guilt, but from frustration and a sense that they must cope alone. This leads to feelings of inadequacy and despair.

Certainly, in most cases they do not wish the State or society to take all the weight from their shoulders. However, they are ready to admit that there are some sections of their child's development which are beyond their knowledge or their experience. It is in such areas that they seek help. They are not seeking an abrogation of responsibility, accountability or love.

In the accounts that we have read, there are no cases where a handicapped child has in any sense divided a family, although in some of them tensions and resentments bubble beneath the surface of the family unit. Some of these resentments are often only declared in retrospect by a father or another child member of the family. But they do reveal the hidden strains that are present even in the most congenial family set-ups. It seems silly to view the presence of a handicapped child in terms of bucolic innocence and sweetness. For every smile there must be a sigh. Anyone seeking to help a mother of a handicapped child ought to be aware that such a mother in all probability will to some extent be emotionally vulnerable. She is going to think with her heart and no one should deny her doing that.

It would be strange indeed if any mothers in this type of situation did not express some anger from time to time. Indeed, it would seem that this would be essential for them if they are going to maintain their sanity throughout the years ahead of them. The aggression when it is expressed is usually borne of frustration, and (I know this only too well) a professional worker in this field will give an understatement with a view to progress, treatment and prognosis for the future of a handicapped child. Optimism is pruned so that expectation will not soar beyond the bounds of reality. This is fair enough, to give false hopes of achievement and progress would be wicked and dangerous. However, there is a danger of too much pruning of hopes and it would seem relevant that the professional worker in the field should combine his heart with his head. I remember talking to a headteacher nearing retirement. She had to relay some terrible information to a mother concerning the mother's child.

'I got up at four that morning. I couldn't sleep you know, Mrs . . . wasn't due in school until ten-thirty. I've been at this a long time, but you can't deny your feelings can you? We had a cup of tea together and then I told her the lot, all of it. Just what to expect. I had to. Well, she cried. Then I cried. We put our arms around one another and sobbed. After that we talked and worked things out quietly. It wasn't that one felt that much more relieved, but one felt that much more human. In other words, I had stopped merely observing and advising and become me.'

One of the main problems that stands in the way of shedding enlightenment to parents is that with babies or very young children it is often extremely difficult for all the professional workers concerned to come to any composite conclusions. In the main, forecasts are hazarded where a prognosis is what the parents ask for. To be fair to the helper or worker, it is an unenviable position to be in, particularly when prognosis varies enormously between individual children. All mongol children are not just mongol and that is an end to the future. There is enormous variability in terms of performance of different children even in such a fierce inheritant syndrome as the Downes one. Therefore bad news or chilling news needs to be tempered with some reassurance and a great deal of encouragement.

When one considers the alternatives one has to accept the premise that hope must be offered in one way or another. Mothers who become part of this minority group within our society have two options – one is hope and one is apathy. As long as the hope is not fully satisfied, there will be some aggression and one should be thankful for it. However, if apathy sets in, then surely this must lead towards the first steps of neglect and then abandonment. Yet even in harsh economic times, unless parents in this position have recourse to what can only be called reasonable support, hope, however strong, will diminish and in

85

this process suffering and turmoil will spill deeper into the family. This is not to say that every mother wishes the State to take her by the hand. There are some politicians and economists (not afflicted by handicap) who shriek 'expense, expense' and make empty clarion calls to voluntary bodies and charities as a panacea to answer all ills and needs.

History makes it abundantly clear that if voluntary organisations had not sprung up the advancement of work on behalf of the handicapped would have progressed much less than it has at present. Present provision still causes alarm and worry to the aware. Without the tenacity of purpose that voluntary organisations continue to engender, present provision and facilities would be much leaner and more spare than they are now. We have to be curiously thankful that handicap cuts across and weaves itself into all kinds of family background. It can be the integrating force for a group of people who are otherwise alien to one another on religious, political or cultural terms.

Local branches of voluntary organisations are practical and useful in that they actually do exist. A recurrent theme when one meets mothers of the handicapped goes something like this: 'I'll talk it over with Anita and some of the others, we are meeting at her house next week . . .' or 'You know it's not only Lisa, I met a marvellous couple at the meeting on Wednesday, you can't believe what they have gone through with their son. His illness started at university, he has been at home for the last four years . . . it's not that you go to hear stories of parallel suffering with your own, it's just that if someone has experienced something similar to you they *know* how you feel.' Apart from offering this clear empathy voluntary organisations are often responsible for funding both provision and research in all types of handicap from a relatively common one to the more rare. It is imperative that the dialogue between the State and such societies continues to exist. One can only view with the deepest sadness the present financial plight of so many societies and voluntary organisations which have for years contributed so much to what would have remained unsung areas of provision. In this sense, we hear of firms, factories, opera houses, all kinds of places rescued by State aid. The intent of such rescue operations is that they will eventually return the investment in terms of employment and production. Given these terms of reference it is difficult to see how some charities are allowed to die when the needs that they are answering are proven beyond doubt. In the main these charities did not come into being from groups of pithy sentimentalists, nor from aged local councillors searching for an OBE epitaph. They were born of searing needs and of individuals recognising them and attempting to heal or assuage them in one way or another.

Understanding and awareness of the handicapped is still limited to so few people and it is here that education can help. Education of all children in all schools, education of the families that have a handicapped child in their midst, and education of the public. The last of these sections is possibly the largest area and certainly the leanest in terms of awareness. Where does one begin? It really does need something tantamount to an assault course in approaching government ministries concerned with housing, employment, leisure and sport. Please note that health and social services have been left from the assault as rape is constantly being advocated for that particular ministry and one fears for its survival. None of these ministries should act in isolation with regard to help for the handicapped. However, a cohesive approach or plan does not appear to be even in its conception stage.

This situation has probably arisen from ignorance or from individuals failing to explain needs correctly or imbue the sense of urgency that they feel about meeting these needs satisfactorily. Enlisting help is one thing, maintaining it is another. Explanation is difficult and is often hidden beneath jargon. The problems of explaining a handicap to the mother of an afflicted child are difficult to say the least. All the mothers in this book can bear testament to that and there are many, many more. Are there any guide-lines to explanation? It would seem that most mothers on discovering that their child is handicapped, whether the handicap is congenital or is one that manifests itself later, suffer shock, bewilderment and grief.

As far as a marriage or a family is concerned, this appears to have one effect or another. In some cases it brings the parents and the rest of the family closer together. They appear to draw upon each others' strength as if they were in a state of siege, their loyalty towards each other seems more intense and impregnable. However, it would seem that these marriages or families

are reasonably happy and stable before the advent of a handicapped child, and the child concerned only reinforces and
heightens qualities in the relationship which were already there
in the first instance. On the other hand, marriages that are not
so firmly based seem to deteriorate further. In these instances I
have found that it is the mother who is left with the added stress
of the difficult prospects of caring for her child. Both child and
mother suffer accordingly and father opts for a course of with-
drawal and sustained isolation from the situation confronting
him. I could have written about many mothers in this situation – but would it have helped them? Also, if you are involved
with helping and working with such mothers, you cannot
pseudonymise them away by referring to them as Mrs X or Mrs
Z. There comes a point where objectivity, or call it what you
will, must be sacrificed.

'I just could not believe it. No, this couldn't happen to me.
Why should it happen to me? It is a bad dream, no, a bloody
nightmare, I'll wake up and. . . .' Parental reactions appear to
be similar after the shock and bewilderment. All of them seem
to experience or demonstrate denial of what has come about. In
most instances it is merely time which disintegrates this denial.
It can extend for weeks, months or even years. Fortunately,
realisation comes gently and reasonably swiftly for most; when
it does come the issues involved are still very hard to bear and
sadness pervades the mother.

I don't think that this sadness should be tampered with unless
it leads to depression or despair. In most cases the sadness seems
to be broken by anger. 'I've had my fill of crying, I could mope
all day. I am going to get something done about it.' This impetus
carries them forward – they question, they cajole, they sometimes shout in their searches for help. They may appear irrational to some cold professional eyes, but for most of them this
stage is fundamental to their eventual adaptation to their situation.

'Well sometimes when you come across someone who has been
really cruel, you have a choice of either laughing or crying at the
situation. I have learned to laugh at a good many things that
might have upset me in the early years. The reaction of some
people, even of relatives, to a handicapped child is really tragic.
I mean for them, not for me, or sometimes it's unbearably

hypocritical, you learn to recognise why some people have to deliver hurt arrows. Your skin gets thicker and the arrows bounce off you after a time. But I suppose some of them leave their marks. As far as friendships go – you only have time for the real ones. Yes, you accept things and just get on with it, you count your own injuries less, but I suppose some of them will always be there.'

The 'marks' or 'injuries' that this particular mother mentions do seem to remain and do affect the mothers in some cases. After the initial stages of shock and grief they are confronted with, first, a period of inactive sadness, second, a period of frantic search for the best help or even a 'magic cure'. Many are subjected to years of stress; this can increase as a child gets older, depending on the severity of the handicap or whether or not it is of a progressive nature. At one time I was teaching a haemophiliac infant of seven or eight years who had been placed (quite correctly) in a school for physically handicapped children. 'When he was a baby it was so much easier. I mean, he looked all right and as long as we kept our eye on him, things weren't too bad. But now it's that much harder, although we know what to expect. The older he gets, the harder it is. He's taken after his older brothers, he loves football. If he plays it, it will eventually be the death of him. If I have to stop him playing, it could be the death of me. My nerves are shattered.' Nervous exhaustion and physical debility are symptoms which affect not only the mothers, but also workers and helpers in this field. Stress sheds like pollen and the emotionally fatigued seem to be more vulnerable to it than most. In this instance, emotions need to be reorganised; that is not to say that they should in any way be denied.

One supposes that there is always a certain amount of routine and ritual in every household. This is a structural development that comes about to contribute to the corporate happiness of the household and on occasions demands varying amounts of personal sacrifice on behalf of individual inmates. In a family where a handicapped child is present the sacrifices are probably greater and the routines and rituals more fierce. This does cause resentment from other members of the family from time to time and one cannot be too judgmental of this resentment in the light of some of the circumstances to which they are subjected.

Very often the resentment is buried and held back and not expressed until years later.

'I suppose it wasn't until I was married myself that I realised what Mum had to put up with. Sometimes I would hurt her in sly little ways because I thought she was giving more time to . . . than me. I would make an excuse to go out and leave her to do the washing up just to punish her. I knew why I was doing it, but I couldn't stop myself. I've since wondered whether she realised it or not – we have talked about it since and she isn't angry and says she understands it. I love my Mum.'

A total dedication of all their time for their handicapped child does not appear to appeal to most mothers that I have known. This is probably demonstrated more vividly by the needs of helpers such as teachers, doctors, social workers, health visitors, who all reach peaks of fatigue: 'I'm desperate to get away from it all, I'll feel better after holidaying'; 'I go fishing on a Sunday – and by watching that float, I forget everything for a time'; 'Sometimes when I get home I say to myself, switch off, forget, but it is not as easy as it sounds. The only way I know when I have switched off, I mean really switched off, is when I begin to notice and appreciate little things like Christmas decorations – it's as though my sense of wonder had returned. Sounds a bit childish doesn't it?'

The routines in many homes make allowances for leisure of one kind or another. This contributes towards the well-being of all the family. Where any form of leisure is denied by circumstance or by the sheer intensity of demand it seems likely that all are going to suffer. A total denial of leisure and wonderment can eventually be the initial steps towards child neglect. When this occurs how easy it seems to lay blame. Blaming someone seems to come much more easily than helping someone – particularly after the event. 'I suppose it's my own fault, I did tend to pay less attention to Mary because Barbara needed more of my time. If I hadn't done that then . . .;' or, 'Yes, I have contacted everyone and still got nowhere with the referral. I really blasted the clerk at the office and I gave the medical department the worst part of my tongue.' The simplest way of opting out of accountability and responsibility is to blame someone else or even bring blame on to ourselves. When the blame is laid it seems to fulfil the instant appetite of a gawping cormorant that someone may have identified as need. It does nothing to satisfy the cormorant's deep and abiding hunger – only help can do that and such help is not solely concerned with cause and effect.

It is at this point that feelings cannot be placed in abeyance or abrogated. Most people working in caring situations have been lacerated by one colleague or another and have delivered wounds to people they respect and love for this very reason. At present, where all administrations seem to be getting larger, there is a danger of conflict arising between the worker in the field (who by definition must be parochial to be effective) and the bastions of administration, hierarchy and local government agencies whose support they are dependent on. At times, this can make the helper feel very lonely, quite often this can cause the helper to feel boxed and strangled when he needs to be liberated in order to help. All structures should seek to see that these feelings are not engendered.

I had cause to see the Chief Staff Inspector of Special Education. I needed help. I had known this woman for many years and had watched her career progress. It would be difficult for anyone who had worked with her to begrudge her achievements and to feel that she was in any way unworthy of her present position. She had worked in the field, she was experienced and managed to combine wisdom with tenderness. In spite of being aware of these qualities, in spite of my admiration of this woman, I viewed the interview with trepidation. The long corridors did nothing to allay my fears and feelings of insecurity. It was the status, not the person that caused these feelings. Perhaps I felt the status might have changed the person. I don't know.

I waited in the office, she came in looking slightly flustered, she had been solving some problem with someone in the corridor. She answered the telephone twice in ten minutes. She dealt with three 'pressing' appointments, gave dates, times, etc. Answered a letter or two, apologised to me for not giving her time to me immediately. I noticed that her dress was wrongly buttoned, she had not had time to notice it.

'I order all my clothes from mail order firms. I just look at the pictures and put a tick next to A, B, C or D.' She smiled. 'I just don't, or can't, make the time for shopping.'

Looking at her, listening to her, gave me confidence. I would talk to her and not her nomenclature. I talked. Within a short time it was clear that my apprehensions and fears were unfounded, I was talking to the person not the status. She listened to me with intent and her rejoinders indicated the depth of her understanding with regard to my particular problem. What was more important, two hours after I had been with her, she took me for dinner. In the restaurant she offered more than food, more than understanding, she offered compassion.

'I feel so very sorry for the poor dears. I was just compelled to do something – and I feel quite proud of my achievements in my quiet little way.'

I would not want to be critical of the statement, I think it echoes many of the sentiments that helping agencies of those working with the handicapped initially experience. You have pity on what you see, you act accordingly and proffer help in whatever way you can, but you also feel better that you are doing something good. After a while another dawning occurs; whereas pity can be flashed on (or off for that matter) like a light bulb, compassion comes more slowly, it is more hazardous because you not only view the suffering, but share it. There are no rewards here, you help or give in the same way that you breathe, in the same way that your heart continues to beat. It is total in itself. The person giving help is on an equal footing with the person being helped.

On the other hand, pity elevates the giver's position. With this elevation it is impossible to avoid being like a large fort that is prevented from opening its drawbridge by the moat surrounding it. Compassion lets down the drawbridge – creates areas for entrance and reduces the state of siege that so many would-be helpers may quickly find themselves. If it is realised, then the fears that large organisations will become uncaring, or remote from the parochialism of what each individual is concerned with, would (for the most part) be groundless.

'Thank you, Marie,' I said.

'For what?' she asked.

'Feeding me,' I said.

I insisted on paying the bill, perhaps she was puzzled about my goodnight response, the food that she had given needed neither preparation nor cooking, it had flowed from her with ease and naturalness, no amount of power, hierarchal position, political position, can poison or pollute this. If enough people received it and gave it then one has to be forced to accept that the future outlook for us all would be optimistic. For these reasons I do not believe that any great political or religious hierarchies can achieve much in the alleviation of suffering with regard to the human condition. Hope must rest in the self-realisation and awareness of individuals whose enlightenment slashes away the postured care of communities, bureaucracies and establishments even if the individuals concerned are part of those groupings. Compassion remains beyond threat.

Let May, Rose, Babs and Margaret feed you a little and accept some hope. Inevitably, you will pass it along sometime in some place.

Z